Murder & Crime: Grimsby

Murder & Crime: Grimsby

By Douglas Wynn

Frontispiece: Grimsby Docks in the early 1900s. (Stuart Sizer)

Publisher's note: Owing to the nature of the subject matter, please be aware that some readers may find the content of this book disturbing.

First published in 2007 by Tempus Publishing
Reprinted 2008

Reprinted in 2009 by
The History Press
The Mill, Brimscombe Port,
Stroud, Gloucestershire, GL5 2QG
www.thehistorypress.co.uk

© Douglas Wynn, 2009

The right of Douglas Wynn to be identified as the Author of this work has been asserted in accordance with the Copyrights, Designs and Patents Act 1988.

All rights reserved. No part of this book may be reprinted or reproduced or utilised in any form or by any electronic, mechanical or other means, now known or hereafter invented, including photocopying and recording, or in any information storage or retrieval system, without the permission in writing from the Publishers.

British Library Cataloguing in Publication Data.
A catalogue record for this book is available from the British Library.

ISBN 978 07524 4295 2

Typesetting and origination by
Tempus Publishing Limited.

Contents

	Acknowledgements	6
	Introduction – Crime in Grimsby	7
one	Richard Insole – Shots in the Night	9
two	Alice Harper – 'I Never Touched It'	15
three	Joseph Woodhall – A Moment of Madness	19
four	Henry Rumbold – Nothing like an Old Fool	27
five	Hayter and Ostler – A Tragic Love Story	35
six	Charles Smith – A Lethal Triangle	41
seven	George Turner – The Errant Wife	47
eight	William Hall – Revenge is not Sweet	53
nine	Samuel Smith – The Evils of Drink	59
ten	The Ridlington Brothers – Slaughter by Saucepan	65
eleven	William Wright – In Trouble with Mr Wright	71
twelve	Norah Walker – The Cup that Kills	79
thirteen	Daniel Revell – Act of Murder	87
	Bibliography	95

Acknowledgements

My thanks are due to the many people who have helped me with this book, but especially I would like to thank the staff of Lincoln Central Library, the reference library staff at Grimsby Library and the staff at Louth Library and Mablethorpe Library, in particular Kathryn Whitehead for being so patient with me. I should also like to thank Margaret Tinkler for helping with research and the loan of books and David N. Robinson for helpful discussions and information, for permission to quote from his book *The Lincolnshire Seaside* and for the very generous loan of pictures from his collection. My thanks are also due to Norman Cawkwell and Stuart Sizer for the loan of pictures from their collections. I am also grateful to the editor of the *Grimsby Telegraph* for permission to use line drawings and part of the text from issues of the *Grimsby Evening Telegraph* and the *Grimsby News* and to the editor of *The Louth Leader* for permission to use part of the text of an issue of the *Louth and North Lincolnshire Advertiser*. Last but certainly not least, I should like to thank my wife Rosemary who helped greatly with the research and shared with me the ups and downs which a project like this entails. Without her help and encouragement the book would not have been completed.

Introduction
Crime in Grimsby

Grimsby was founded in the late 800s by Danish settlers, one of whom was called Grim or Grimmr and it became known as Grims-by, *by* being the Danish word for village. By 1086 Grimsby had a population of 200 to 250 and the land on which it stood was owned by William the Conqueror's half-brother, Bishop Odo of Bayeux.

It was important because it was on a tidal creek of the Humber River, called the Haven, and sheltered by the hills in what is now Cleethorpes. There were also some fresh water springs nearby. It was a good place for ships to call at and for vessels to fish from, for the Humber and the North Sea at the time were full of fish. Grimsby thus developed into a busy port. Wine was brought in from France and Spain, wood from Norway and coal came down the coast from Newcastle, whereas wool was exported from Grimsby.

Grimsby had its charter from King John in 1201. The population was then between 1,500 and 2,000. It had a mayor, its own local government and its own court. At about this time Emot Marshall, a servant, was put in the stocks (a device for securing the legs) for leaving her master's service without permission. Katherine Wilson was pilloried, her arms and neck placed into a wooden structure, and drawn round the town for being a scold. In comparison, Elizabeth Brown was given a week to leave town for keeping a brothel.

To deal with such transgressions and many others besides, Grimsby had its own town watch. This comprised bailiffs, constables and petty constables. In 1404 there were three petty constables for Brighowgate and Wellowgate, three for the market, one for Baxtergate and two for North St Marygate. Parish constables were appointed for a year. They were unpaid, received no proper training and had to report to the magistrates at each quarter session. It was not a popular job and could often be a dangerous one as well. It is recorded that one night in 1434 two men of the town watch tried to arrest Robert Tevelby. He drew a dagger and shot an arrow at them but they finally cornered and captured him at a house near the Haven.

By the late fifteenth century, the Haven had begun to silt up. For nearly 300 years the population continued to decline and Grimsby became little more than a village with a market. Coal was still imported however and grain from the surrounding countryside exported and so in 1556 the wooden bridge over the Haven was replaced by a stone one. Late in the 1700s trade began to pick up and a turnpike road was built to Wold Newton.

George Kilpike, a chimney sweep, was accused at Lincoln Assizes in July 1788 of highway robbery. He is said to have threatened the life of a young woman who was milking a cow in a field at the village of Waltham and robbed her of eighteen pence. Kilpike's alibi, that he was in bed at the time, was supported by his landlady. However, the jury did not believe them. His landlady was charged with perjury and Kilpike was convicted and hanged.

At the time more than 200 offences including forgery and coining as well as robbery, rape and murder, were capital offences, although many death sentences were not carried out. Around half of those condemned to death at Lincoln Assizes might be reprieved, being sentenced instead to be transported for life. Property crime was treated more seriously. Rapists and murderers were often reprieved, but robbers and those stealing horses were invariably hanged.

In 1801 Grimsby had a population of 1,524 and was comparable in size to Market Rasen, Louth, Horncastle and Caistor. By 1831 the population was just over 4,000, but by the end of the century it had climbed to 75,000. Around 1800 a new dock and quays had been built and the Haven deepened. Yet the real impetus to the expansion of Grimsby was the coming of the railways. Grimsby had been a small fishing port for many years, but most of the fishing vessels operating in the North Sea landed their catches at Hull, which had better communications with the rest of the country. The sailing vessels were called smacks and in 1845 there were forty smacks fishing out of Hull. However, in calm weather the smacks had to be towed down the Humber to the open sea and fish landed at Hull had to be taken further up the Humber to the first river bridge at Goole in order for them to be sold in the south. When the railways came to Grimsby it was much quicker to land fish there to feed the southern markets.

Grimsby acquired its first 'lock-up', instituted to deter vagrants from visiting the town, in 1845 and in 1856 the Rural Police Act compelled authorities to set up police forces in country areas. In the early Victorian era rape cases were often treated lightly, but in 1866 a case occurred which showed that attitudes were hardening. Lucy Sizer was a sixteen-year-old servant girl who was coming home from chapel on 13 May 1866 when she was assaulted by a man named Crawford outside the dock offices. He dragged her into a shed in the railway yard where she was attacked by four other youths. She recognised one and he was subsequently arrested and informed on the other four. All five were convicted of rape. Crawford got fifteen years and the other four six years each.

This book is a compilation of murders and alleged murders which took place in Grimsby and the surrounding area between 1831 and 1949. Although the stories are true and every effort has been made to stick to the facts I have inserted conversations in places. These are true records of what was said, based on newspaper reports of the inquests, committal reports and trials, and I have only updated them when the old-fashioned speech sounds a little stilted to our modern ears.

William Congreve said, 'see how love and murder will out'. And I hope that these stories show that they nearly always do.

one

Richard Insole
Shots in the Night

It was about 9.45 p.m. on a Friday night in January 1887 when the front door of a little house in Wellington Terrace, Grimsby, opened and a young woman came in from the darkness outside. In the flickering light of an oil lamp placed on a table in the front room, the young woman's face showed fear. She trembled slightly, looking back over her shoulder for the young man following her. The reason for her fear became immediately apparent, for in his right hand he carried a revolver. It was pointed at her.

The young woman stumbled through into the back kitchen where her mother and father were sitting. They immediately jumped to their feet as they saw the young man behind their daughter and what he was carrying in his hand.

'Oh, Dick! What have you come for?' said her mother in a trembling voice.

'I am come like a man,' replied the young man firmly.

The older couple looked a bit puzzled at the reply, but the older man had seemingly summed up the situation for he began sidling round the wall of the room to get to the door. The young man seemed not to notice as he gazed steadily at the young woman. But her mother had seen her husband move out of the corner of her eye and she said quickly, 'Annie, what's the matter?'

The young woman hung her head and mumbled something her mother could not hear, but the distraction had allowed her father to slip out of the door behind the young man. He crept out of the front door and set off to find a policeman.

'I want an answer,' grated the young man, waving the pistol menacingly.

He seemed agitated himself and in the flickering candle light his face looked pale and sweaty.

Annie gulped and when her voice came it was hoarse and scratchy. 'If... if you will go outside for ten minutes, I will tell you.'

'No. That won't do for me. I want it now.'

And he raised the revolver and pointed it at Annie's head.

Her voice now was shaky. Indeed her whole body was shaking. 'I... I will come back to you.'

But this did not satisfy the young man. He jerked the gun peremptorily and his face took on a cruel look. 'I want another kind of answer.'

Perhaps it was because the young man had done nothing with the gun in his hand so far except to wave it about that the young woman took some courage from this. At all events, her chin jutted out and firmness appeared on her face.

A fishing smack of the kind that Richard Insole might have sailed in. (David N. Robinson)

'I can't give it,' she said quietly.
'Who is guilty? You or I?'
'I can't answer that.'
'There's a James Shepherd between us.'
The young woman said nothing, but she raised her head and looked at the young man.
'Never mind,' he said. 'I'll do it now.'
And he pulled the trigger.

The young man's name was Richard Insole. He was twenty-four years old and an apprentice fisherman, being second or third hand on a fishing smack. He was articled to Mr John Guzzwell who owned several fishing vessels. The apprentice system for fishermen in Grimsby in the late nineteenth century followed the rapid expansion of the fishing trade. At this time, the demand for hands to man the fishing smacks and later the steam trawlers was heavy. In the 1880s and 1890s well over half the crew members would be apprentices. They were often recruited from the workhouses and reformatories of the larger cities and their ages ranged from twelve to twenty-five. Life was exceedingly hard for the boys who were often undernourished, ill-clad and inexperienced. A common cause of death was a boy following orders to fling a bucket over the side of the vessel on a rope to obtain water to wash the deck. The pull of a rough sea on the rope would often be enough to jerk the lad overboard and he would be lost. Beatings from the skippers were common and desertions by the boys often occurred, when they were punished by imprisonment.

Richard Insole seems to have been a disobedient young lad. In March 1875 when he was twelve, Insole was brought before the magistrates for neglect of duty and given a warning. In September of the same year he was convicted of disobedience and served twenty-one days in prison. Two years later he got a month and two months after that he went to prison for five weeks again for disobedience. In July 1878 when he was fifteen, he served time for neglect of duty.

He married Sarah Ann Robinson in 1881, when he was eighteen and she was seventeen and then he seems to have settled down for a period. But Mr Guzzwell described him as a young man of 'passionate temper' and, although not addicted to drink as many fishermen were, he still indulged in fits of violence. In July 1886 he was convicted of assaulting his wife and sentenced to six weeks of hard labour. His wife left him and went to live with her parents at 41 Wellington Terrace, which was a short road leading off Wellington Street between Freeman Street and what is now Albion Street. When Insole was released he was brought before the bench again on an application by his wife for maintenance, and an order for 7s 6d per week made against him for the support of his wife and their child.

At the inquest, which was held in the boardroom of the hospital and at which Richard Insole was present, Annie's mother, Mrs Robinson, described how her daughter had returned from her shift at the fish house at just before ten o'clock and Richard Insole had followed her in brandishing a pistol. As he fired the first shot her daughter knocked his hand up and cried, 'Oh Dick, don't!' He fired again and she collapsed against a chair. Mrs Robinson bravely tried to come between them but he flung her away with great violence and continued firing at the prostrate figure collapsed on the floor by the fireplace, even going so far as to bend over and fire directly at his wife's chest. Then he put the revolver down on the table and Mrs Robinson thought he was going to reload it. Instead, he picked it up again and rushed out of the house.

Mr Robinson arrived soon after with PC Brocklesby and Sergeant Martin, closely followed by Dr Grimoldby. In his evidence, the doctor said that four shots had hit the unfortunate woman; one hit her right forearm, one her collar bone and two others her chest, one above and one

Grimsby Hospital where the inquest on Sarah Ann Robinson was held. (David N. Robinson)

below her left breast. The last two had been the fatal wounds and the poor woman had died on the floor before he arrived. Sergeant Martin reported that the revolver was a six-chambered weapon and one round had been left in the cylinder. Insole had missed once, but the other four rounds had found their mark.

When Insole left he rushed to his mother's house at 44 Albion Street, just round the corner, and there stabbed himself with a kitchen knife in the lower chest. The knife however struck a rib and did little damage, inflicting a wound that was only an inch deep. He was apprehended there later that night by PC Brocklesby. Sergeant Martin arrived shortly afterwards.

The sergeant said that he got a cab to carry the prisoner away and during the ride Insole said, 'Take me to my wife.'

Sergeant Martin replied, 'You are going to see a doctor. You will be taken to the police station and there will be charged with murdering your wife by shooting her.'

'I own I did it. She first said she would live with me and then she would not promise before it was too late.'

Another witness at the inquest was Margaret Ellens, wife of William Ellens, a fish carter. She was a sister of Sarah Insole and heavily pregnant. She, too, was living with her mother in Wellington Terrace and occupied the front room of the house. She had seen her sister come in that night followed by Insole and had heard the conversation between the prisoner and her sister.

She was asked by the foreman of the jury who James Shepherd was. She replied that he had been a great friend of Richard Insole (she turned to indicate the prisoner when she said this) but that Insole had become jealous of him all at once. At this the prisoner nodded his head. 'Yes, I caught them in the act of adultery.'

Insole was asked if he wanted to question any witness, but answered that he didn't. And when asked if he wanted to say anything, he replied that he did not. After a few minutes of deliberation, the jury brought in a verdict of wilful murder against Richard Insole.

Subsequently he was committed by the Grimsby magistrates for trial at the Lincoln Assizes. The murder trial opened on Monday 31 January 1887 before Mr Justice Field and the prosecution was in the hands of Mr Etherington Smith and Mr Craycroft. The prisoner pleaded not guilty and the defence was undertaken by Mr Harris.

He had a difficult job. Insole had already confessed his crime to Sergeant Martin and there were witnesses to the shooting to confirm his statement. In addition, Mr Wolfe Abraham, a second-hand dealer of Strand Street, Grimsby, told how on the afternoon of the shooting, Insole came into his shop and bought a revolver which he had seen in the shop window. The price was 7s, but Insole paid only six asking the witness to trust him with the other shilling until he returned later on.

Mrs Elizabeth Hobson, the wife of an ironmonger of Victoria Street, Grimsby, reported that the prisoner came into their shop on the same afternoon and bought fifty cartridges. He brought the revolver with him to try loading it with one of the cartridges.

All this indicated that the crime was premeditated, a requisite for a murder conviction, making it difficult for Mr Harris to provide an adequate defence. He pointed out that Insole was deeply attached to his wife and on returning home from sea, had found that she had betrayed him with another man. At that time the prisoner was not allowed to give evidence himself. Mr Harris proposed to read a statement made by Insole, but was asked to hand it to the judge who would read it and pass on to the jury anything he thought might be in the prisoner's favour. Mr Harris also said that he had some witnesses who would prove that the deceased had received visits from a man named Shepherd, but was advised by the judge not to call them.

Greetwell Road Prison, Lincoln, today.

The judge summed up strongly against the prisoner, saying that he had never heard of a worse case in the whole of his experience and there was nothing in the evidence to justify a verdict of manslaughter.

The jury expressed a desire to retire to consider their verdict. The judge then said that he did not see why they needed to retire unless it was to discuss a recommendation for mercy. The jury duly retired and brought in a verdict of guilty of murder with a recommendation of mercy. The judge asked on what grounds they recommended mercy. The jury replied that it was on grounds of the wife's infidelity. The judge retorted that this was no justification for the crime and forbade the jury from passing such a recommendation. The jury retired again and this time brought in a recommendation of mercy on the grounds of provocation. Mr Justice Field pronounced the sentence of death by hanging and the prisoner had to be helped from the court.

In those days there was no appeal system, but Mr John Barker, Insole's solicitor, raised a petition for the reprieve of the condemned man, urging that, 'the sad and profligate life of the deceased which was a matter of general notoriety in the neighbourhood where the parties resided was the chief provocation to the committal of the murder and such as to justify Her Majesty in exercising her prerogative of mercy'. This was signed by the Bishop of Lincoln, the clergy and nonconformist ministers of Grimsby, several magistrates and members of the town council and 4,000 residents of the town.

The petition was presented at the Home Office by Mr Heneage, MP for the borough, but the Home Secretary saw no grounds for Her Majesty interfering with the carrying out of the sentence. And on the morning of Monday 21 February at Lincoln Prison in Greetwell Road, as the cathedral bell 'Big Tom' boomed out the sixth note of nine o'clock, the hangman, James Berry, pulled the lever which sent twenty-four-year-old Richard Insole to his death.

two

ALICE HARPER

'I Never Touched It'

Lime Street in Grimsby used to run from Chantry Lane in the West Marsh to Haven Terrace, which runs alongside the river Freshney, crossing Lord Street about halfway along its length. Now only the half between Lord Street and Haven Terrace exists. The rest is occupied by Bemrose Way. Yet it was in this southern half, at number 16 Lime Street, that Mrs Alice Harper lived in 1901. She was a widow in her forties with a thirteen-year-old daughter. Her husband had died about four years before and she had taken in a lodger. In May of that year there were just the three, Alice Harper, her daughter and the lodger, living at number 16.

On the evening of the 17th of that month Alice Harper went to see Dr John Bruce at his surgery in Town Hall Square. She complained of a pain in her side as well as a swelling which she thought might be a tumour. Since Dr Bruce could not fully examine her that evening, he agreed to see her at her home the next day. There, the doctor made a more careful investigation. After he had done so, he took off his stethoscope and put it away in his black bag.

'It's good news in a way, Mrs Harper. You haven't got a tumour. But not in another; you are pregnant.'

Alice Harper, who had been lying on her bed, sat up in alarm and her face went white.

'I don't know what I shall do,' she wailed. 'I have been trying to earn a respectable living since my husband died. Now I shall lose all my custom.'

She was right to be worried. In the Edwardian period there were few things more socially disastrous than a baby born out of wedlock. Young girls from wealthy families, if they became pregnant and had sympathetic parents, could be packed off to the country where they could be hidden away until the baby was born. Then arrangements would be made to have it secretly adopted. Less sympathetic or less affluent parents might even throw the girl out for having brought disgrace to the family. Alternatively, she might be sent to a home for unmarried mothers.

A middle-aged mother might not suffer this fate, but she would certainly be ostracised. Alice Harper, who worked as a cleaner and had her own customers would rapidly lose them and would find it difficult, if not impossible, to obtain other employment.

The doctor was sympathetic. He knew that she had only a few weeks to go before the birth and he realised that she would in great difficulties then. He listened while she poured out her story.

'I was being courted by a man,' she said tearfully, 'and he forced me against my will.'

He didn't tell her that if it was true it constituted rape and if she had come forward at the time it might have mitigated her situation. But all that he could do was to ensure that the birth

Lime Street where Alice Harper lived, as it looks today.

was accomplished with the least stress and danger to the mother and child. He fully expected to be called to the confinement. But he wasn't.

On Friday 21 June Alice Harper went to work in the early morning as usual, cleaning some offices before the occupants arrived. She took her young daughter with her. At thirteen, the child could well have left school or possibly not even attended one. In 1905 there were twelve elementary schools in Grimsby and one higher grade school, but attendance was not compulsory.

During the morning Alice began to feel unwell and she told her daughter that she would have to go home. The daughter followed a few minutes later. It is very probable that Alice Harper knew that the birth was imminent, for when she reached home she rushed upstairs and sat on a chamber pot. When her daughter arrived and heard her mother moaning she too dashed up to her mother's bedroom. But her mother had shut the door and would not open it. Even at this late stage, such was the stigma of an illegitimate birth that she was desperate not to let her daughter know what was happening. She shouted through the door, telling her daughter to go for Dr Bruce and tell him that her mother had an inflammation or a bleeding abscess.

The doctor said that he received the message at 8.45 a.m. that morning but was unable to go until noon. When he did arrive, he found Alice Harper in bed.

She said, 'I am in a dreadful fix. My baby was born between half past seven this morning and eight and I had no one with me. I felt queer this morning when I came home from the offices and went upstairs to lie down. When I got upstairs I was taken ill.'

She then went on to describe the birth of her child. She continued, 'My daughter heard me making a noise and came up. I told her to go down. I then tided things up and got into bed. I never touched the child at anytime. I hope I won't get into trouble over this.'

Dr Bruce found a bucket under the bed. It contained a chamber pot which was covered with a piece of carpet. He removed the carpet and saw that the chamber pot contained the body of a baby. Only the back was visible as it was lying face down and curled up. He lifted it out and found that it was the dead body of a female baby.

Alice Harper said, 'How can it be buried without my daughter knowing anything about it? I had intended to go away from home on Monday to my sister's, so that it might be born there.'

'I'm afraid I cannot give you a certificate for the burial of the child and I shall have to get in touch with the coroner.'

Alice Harper began crying. 'I hope you will do the best you can for me. I hope the poor law people will not get to know anything about it.'

The doctor made an examination of Alice Harper to establish that she had in fact just given birth and then he got in touch with the police. Inspector Long and Sergeant Ingleton arrived at Lime Street later that afternoon. By this time, Alice had recovered her composure somewhat. She was sitting up in bed and she said, 'I don't know what all the bother is about. If Dr Bruce had come when I sent for him it would have been alright.'

And she told the two policemen what she had told Dr Bruce. They found the bucket with the chamber pot inside, put away in a cupboard, and they took the body to the hospital mortuary.

Dr Bruce made a post-mortem examination of the body at the mortuary. He reported that the child was fully developed. He found that the lungs had been fully inflated in every part and the stomach contained mucus and air. He was of the opinion that the child had had a separate existence and must have lived at least one minute and probably longer. This was most important, since if the child had been born dead its mother could not be accused of causing its death. He estimated that death was due to two causes: firstly to haemorrhage from the cord and secondly to asphyxiation.

He gave this evidence at the inquest, which was opened on Monday 24 June at the Grimsby Hospital, when sufficient evidence was given to allow the child to be buried and then it was resumed a fortnight later, when Alice Harper was present. After he'd given his evidence, the doctor was asked by a member of the jury if, in his opinion, a medical man or anyone else had been present to render assistance during the birth, would it be likely that the child might have lived? The doctor said he thought in all probability the child would have lived.

At the resumed inquest the doctor's evidence was read over so that Alice Harper could hear it and she asked him why he did not call earlier. He replied that no message had been left at his surgery as to the exact nature of Alice Harper's illness. The message merely said she was suffering from inflammation or an abscess and he had promised to go as soon as he could.

At this point the coroner, Mr Thomas Mountain, pointed out to Alice Harper that she was not represented at the court professionally, which he thought was a pity. Although it was not for him to advise her, he thought that the less she said the better it would be for her. The time might come when she would need professional assistance and although he could not prevent her asking questions if she wished to do so, he thought it would be as well for her to say as little as possible.

Evidence was then given by Alice's daughter who described her mother coming home from work and subsequently taking a message to Dr Bruce's surgery. Inspector Long described his interview with Alice Harper at Lime Street and William Appleby reported receiving the message for Dr Bruce.

The borough coroner then told Alice that she could give evidence to the court if she wished. But he said that he was anxious to be perfectly fair to her in every way and would err on the side of leniency. It was not in his province to give her advice but he would go out of his position and advise her not to make a statement. She wavered a little. Plainly she wanted to say something to justify herself. But in the end she took the coroner's advice and did not make a statement.

The court was then cleared and the jury considered their verdict in private. They deliberated for two and half hours and at the end of that time Alice Harper was brought back into court. The coroner addressed her.

'The jury have unanimously found you guilty of the wilful murder of your infant female child and you now stand committed to take your trial at the next Lincoln Assizes.'

'I never touched it,' said Alice, tears streaming down her face. 'I never touched it.'

Her trial took place at Lincoln on Wednesday 27 November 1901, before Mr Justice Higham. The first Act making it an offence to kill an illegitimate child was passed during the reign of James I and the offence was that of murder. For many years, however, it was recognised that mothers killing newborn babies during periods of depression related to child birth or through incompetence in handling babies, could not be said to have the intent or the premeditation required to substantiate the charge of murder. Thus, many mothers convicted of murdering their offspring were not put to death. But in this country the first Infanticide Act which decreed that a mother who killed her own child of under a year would be charged only with manslaughter, was not passed until 1938.

Mr Bonner who appeared for the Crown said that, with his lordship's permission, he would offer no evidence against the prisoner, as the case chiefly depended upon the evidence of the doctor. The woman had done everything she could before the doctor came, although the doctor felt that had he been present he might have saved the life of the child. The judge thought that that was the proper course as no jury would convict. The jury brought in a verdict of not guilty and Alice Ann Harper walked free.

It would be nice to think that this marked the end of her ordeal but it was probably only the beginning. As Robert Cecil writes in his book *Life in Edwardian England*, 'the crux of Edwardian morality' seems to have been that, 'to those who could avoid being found out almost everything was permitted. Society was ruled by the twin commandments: Thou shalt not have recourse to law; Thou shalt not feature in the popular press.' And, unfortunately, Alice Harper had broken both these commandments.

three

JOSEPH WOODHALL
A Moment of Madness

There was a clatter of breaking glass and the young woman sat up in bed with a jerk. In the dark she fumbled for the matches on the bedside table, struck one and lit the candle in the holder. She looked at her bedside clock. It said ten o'clock. She drew back the covers and sat with her legs over the side of the bed. She could now hear the sound of feet pounding up the stairs. A wave of terror ran through her body. Somebody had obviously broken the glass in the front door, reached in to unlatch it and thus gained access to the house. Was he now coming up the stairs to rape her?

She was young enough to realise that she was very vulnerable here in her bedroom and in her nightdress. This was March 1919 and the war had only been over for a little under five months. There were still soldiers around the narrow streets of Cleethorpes. It wouldn't take much for one of them to take it into his head to break into a house where a young woman was staying alone. Oh how she wished that her mother and her friend had not gone out for the evening.

Would she have time to rush across the room and lock the bedroom door? The pounding feet had reached the landing and she could now hear the man panting after his exertions. Suddenly she relaxed. She recognised the footfalls and knew who the pounding feet belonged to. It was their lodger, Joseph Woodhall. He was fifty years old and she felt quite safe with him. But why had he broken the glass in the front door in order to get in?

Hurriedly she threw on a dressing gown and padded across the floor to the door holding the candle in its holder. By the flickering light she could see Joseph Woodhall standing on the landing taking great gasps of air. His hair was all awry and his eyes were wide and staring.

'Good Heavens, Mr Woodhall. What on earth do you think you are doing, breaking the glass in the front door?'

'I'm sorry Miss Robinson. I had to do it.' He looked about him wildly as if he had never been in the house before and it was strange to him whereas the young woman knew that he had been living in the house on and off for nearly four years.

'Are you all right Mr Woodhall?'

'Yes, yes. Your mother has sent me to get a parcel out of the bathroom.' He pushed past her and went into the bathroom.

'Is mother alright?'

'Yes. Yes,' called Woodhall from the bathroom. 'I left her and Mrs Evans having supper.'

Houses in Mill Road today, where Mrs Robinson lived and Joseph Woodhall lodged.

Miss Robinson went back to her own room, closed the door and sat on the bed. She heard Woodhall go back down the stairs and out of the front door, closing it behind him. Their lodger certainly had looked strange. She remembered that he had gone out earlier in the evening at about six o'clock and returned about nine. He was followed by her mother and her friend Mrs Evans, who lived in Wollaston Road, a few streets away from their own house in Mill Road. The arrangement was that her mother, Mrs Evans and Woodhall were going to spend the evening at Wollaston Road and the two women had left about 9.30 p.m., to be followed a few minutes later by Woodhall. But he had returned after a short while with some chips which he had bought for her at a local shop. Then he had left again, locking up behind him.

He certainly had been behaving strangely lately. That very day she had returned from the office where she worked, to find him vigorously swinging two wooden objects which looked to her like oversized bottles, but which he said were Indian clubs. He explained that it helped to exercise the arms and improve the circulation. He had had the clubs in the house for about a fortnight. She knew too that he had caught malaria during his service with the army in Mesopotamia and still suffered recurrent bouts of the disease. He often complained of severe headaches.

It was no more than half an hour later when there came an insistent banging on the front door. Constance Robinson went down to find Mrs Evans on the doorstep.

'Oh, come! You must come! Your mother has been attacked.'

Mrs Evans was covered in blood and very nearly hysterical, but Constance was able to calm her down a little and get the story from her. Mrs Evans had been struck on the head when she

Wollaston Street today, where Mrs Robinson met her end.

was in her kitchen preparing their supper, she thought by Woodhall. When she came to she found Mrs Robinson lying on the floor in a pool of blood and Woodhall gone. Constance hastily got dressed and went with Mrs Evans back to Wollaston Road. In the hall they found an Indian club heavily stained with blood and in the kitchen they found Mrs Robinson, still unconscious and lying on the floor.

They called Dr McKane, a near neighbour, and he made arrangements for the two women to be taken to hospital. He considered that Mrs Robinson was suffering from compression of the brain due to a fractured skull. Having been shown the Indian club he agreed that it could well have been the weapon used. Mrs Evans also had a head injury but it was much less severe.

Dr Kerry, house surgeon at the hospital, attended Mrs Robinson when she was brought in at a quarter to two on that Saturday morning, 15 March 1919. But the unfortunate lady died while he was dressing her wound. He, too, was of the opinion that her skull had been fractured, but he thought she had received two blows to the back of the head, either of which could have been fatal.

Mrs Sarah Ann Robinson was well known in the district. She came from the Grant family of Cleethorpes and her husband, James William Robinson, had fishing interests in Norfolk. They lived in Mill Road, Cleethorpes, but James Robinson was away from home a good deal. She was an indefatigable charity worker, a prison visitor and ran a room near the sea front dispensing tea, coffee and other refreshments, called the Brighton Street Soldiers' Home. She was also a member of the Grimsby Board of Guardians, who oversaw the running of the workhouse.

Joseph Woodhall had been a sergeant in the 3rd Battalion of the Manchester Regiment.

Brighton Street today, where Mrs Robinson ran a soldiers' home.

This battalion had been posted to Cleethorpes in August 1914 to guard the coastline between Cleethorpes and Tetney Lock and men billeted all over the town. Trenches were dug on the foreshore and at Humberston Fitties and some troops were even stationed on the Humberston Fitties in wooden huts. Woodhall, because of his age and infirmity had been working in the Grimsby Munitions factory in Victoria Street. Mrs Robinson employed a number of people part time to work in her soldiers' home, Mrs Evans being one of them, and over a number of years Woodhall had also given her part time assistance. When the war ended he came to work for her as a full time employee and took up permanent lodgings at Mill Road. He had often stayed there before, having sleeping-out passes from his regiment, although his home was in Wigan, where in Warrington Road he had a wife and five children.

The coroner's inquiry opened at the hospital on Monday 17 March. Evidence of identification was given by Constance Robinson and medical testimony by Dr McKane. Mrs Evans was too ill to attend and the proceedings were adjourned until Monday 31 March. Then Mrs Evans, her head swathed in bandages, told her story.

She described how she and Mrs Robinson arrived at Wollaston Road in the late evening. They both went into the kitchen which was a room at the back of the house with a step down from the passage. While Mrs Robinson sat in her favourite rocking chair, on one side of the door, Mrs Evans began preparing their supper. Woodhall arrived a few moments later and he took a chair on the other side of the door. Soon he complained that he was feeling cold and Mrs Evans told him to draw his chair up nearer to the fire and he did so. Then Mrs Robinson said that she too was cold and Woodhall offered to change places with her, which they did.

Another contemporary view of Brighton Street showing its close proximity to the front at Cleethorpes.

During the evening Woodhall asked Mrs Evans, 'have you such a thing as an old razor of Harry's?'

Harry was Mrs Evans' husband, who was an accountant and away from home at the time.

Mrs Evans searched in some drawers but could not find one and promised to look upstairs when she went to bed that night.

'It would have to be a square-ended one,' said Woodhall.

'He only wants it to pick at a corn,' said Mrs Robinson.

Shortly after this she said in a teasing voice, 'the sergeant is cross with me. He wanted to go home this weekend, but I persuaded him to stay over Sunday.' She then turned to Woodhall. 'But you are going in the morning, aren't you?'

Plainly Woodhall was angry at being ribbed like this.

'No. I am not!' He snapped.

But Mrs Evans would have none of his ill temper.

'Straighten your face out, young man,' she said. 'I don't like to see it like that.'

She turned away and stooped over the fire to attend to the stew she was cooking. Then she was aware of some movement behind her and she heard Mrs Robinson call out.

'Oh Sergeant, you must not hurt Annie!'

Then she herself felt a heavy blow to the back of her head and she lost consciousness. When she came to she was lying on the floor and blood was running down her face. She dragged herself to her feet to see the figure of Mrs Robinson also lying on the floor near the door with her head on the step and blood spreading out over the lino around her. She tried to lift the inert form and get her friend to speak to her, but she could not arouse her, so she staggered to the front door. Woodhall seemed to have gone as the door was open and there was no sign of him. Eventually she managed get herself to Mill Road. Concluding her evidence Mrs Evans admitted that she thought that Woodhall and Mrs Robinson had been great friends and that she had exerted considerable influence over him.

The editor of the *Wigan Observer* received a letter which had been posted in Grimsby on the Saturday morning following the attack. The letter was in an envelope on the outside of which was the word 'confession' and this envelope was in another addressed to the editor. The letter was signed 'Joseph Woodhall, ex-Sgt of 3rd Manchester Regiment, Cleethorpes, Lincolnshire'. Although quite legible it was rather incoherent but contained the flowing passages:

> I never had any liking for a woman until I met Mrs Robinson of Cleethorpes, lady guardian and prison visitor [...] I have been receiving one pound per week to send to my family at 409 Warrington Road, Goose Green, Wigan. At the same time I have worked for it at the Brighton Street Soldiers' Home and at Mill Road saving Mrs Robinson employing a woman at Brighton Street [...] I have sacrificed all for a true woman as I thought in 1914. I was a God fearing man on enlistment and attended the Methodist Free Chapel, Goose Green, Wigan. Now I am a condemned man. I cannot live with the woman I married by law [...] Do not think I am a coward; I am doing this act to save many and leaving five boys to go into the world fatherless.

Cleethorpes front and beach in the 1920s. (David N. Robinson)

Cleethorpes front in the 1920s. (David N. Robinson)

God give them strength to overcome the pitfalls that come their way. These are true facts of a broken-hearted man through a woman.

On the same Saturday evening the station master at Waltham station, William Moore, was surprised to see a strange figure at the ticket widow. He looked dirty and unkempt, his clothes were wet through and he had on no shoes or socks. He told Moore that he had done something wrong. 'I think I have killed somebody,' he said. The station master got in touch with the police, who arrived and arrested Woodhall, for it turned out to be him, but because he looked so ill they took him to the hospital, where he was kept under observation.

Joseph Woodhall was subsequently charged with the murder of Mrs Robinson and brought before the magistrates at the Grimsby County Bench on Saturday 29 March. Although a big man he was so ill, suffering from a bout of malaria, that he had to be supported in the dock by two policemen. He was remanded in custody and eventually committed for trial at Lincoln Assizes.

On Thursday 19 June 1919 he appeared in the Lincoln court looking dazed and rather wild. He was given a chair and leaned his head against a warder at his side as if in pain. Sir Ryland Atkins appeared as prosecutor and the defence was in the hands of Mr Allsebrook who appeared for Woodhall under provisions of the Poor Prisoners' Defence Act. They both said that they felt that Woodhall was unfit to plead and a jury was empanelled to decide the question. Since the prison doctor, Colonel Lambert, was not present, Dr Rotherham of Grimsby was called. He told the court that from observations he had made of the prisoner in March and April, he was of the opinion that he was unfit to plead. However, he was asked to examine him again and Woodhall was taken out of the court for this purpose, shouting and struggling. After a period he returned in the same condition with Dr Rotherham, who confirmed that the prisoner was unfit to plead by the alienation of his mind. The jury quickly brought in a verdict; the prisoner was insane and the judge directed that he should be detained during His Majesty's pleasure.

four

HENRY RUMBOLD
Nothing like an Old Fool

It can surely be only older people, looking back over their lives, who realise the importance of chance in determining events. That dance you went to only on a last-minute decision and met the love of your life. The newspaper left behind by someone in the pub and flicking through it you saw the advertisement for a new job which altered the cause of events so drastically. And the spur of the moment decision to take a new way home which meant you avoided the terrible car smash on your usual route. Was it fate; a benevolent someone up above looking down on you? Or simply that incredible phenomena, pure chance?

Whatever the name we choose to give it, it certainly wasn't benevolent for Henry Edward Rumbold in November 1893 when the main sail of his fishing smack was damaged and he had to return to Grimsby. He could never have guessed that the simple accident would have such tragic consequences.

Rumbold (or, as his name appears in some accounts, 'Rumbell') was born in Yarmouth and at the time of the incident was forty years of age. He had been a fisherman all his life, first in Yarmouth and latterly in Grimsby, and had risen through the ranks from lowly deckhand up to skipper. He was employed by Alderman Henry Smethurst and was the skipper of the trawl-smack *Nightingale*. Skippers could earn good money if they had the knack of being able to find fish in the North Sea and even if they worked as part of a fishing fleet, as Rumbold did, they were still paid by the quantity of fish they landed. Rumbold had been a successful skipper for a number of years and could have been a relatively wealthy man but, like many fishermen he spent his money lavishly and foolishly. He wasn't a heavy drinker, though he liked his glass of spirits. His interests were elsewhere.

Rumbold had left behind in Yarmouth his mother, Mrs Smelton, who was seventy years old, two sisters and a wife. He had been married in his early twenties in Yarmouth and according to him it had lasted only six months, his wife having decamped with all his money when he was at sea. He had several brothers, one of whom shared his lodgings at 50 Stanley Street, Grimsby, on the corner of Duke Street. However, Rumbold's main interest in life when he wasn't at sea was a young lady called Harriet Rushby who was nineteen years old at the time.

Harriet was a native of Grimsby. Her mother, who had been a well-known singer in the town, died when she was young. Harriet appears to have been a wayward young woman. When she was young, she was sent to one of the London homes for lost girls. These were usually for girls who had had children out of wedlock or were uncontrollable at home. It is reported that she returned much improved. She had recently been staying with one of her aunts, Mrs Allan

Above left: Illustration showing Henry Rumbold, taken from the *Grimsby News* for 1 December 1893. (*Grimsby Telegraph*)

Above right: Illustration showing Harriet Rushby, taken from the *Grimsby News* for 1 December 1893. (*Grimsby Telegraph*)

Haywood, but several months before the incident she had left, telling her aunt that she had married Rumbold. This was not the case, although Rumbold did support her; indeed he gave her a great deal of money and was obviously infatuated with her.

Yet he did not trust her to remain faithful to him and in October 1893, before he left on his last voyage he took her to the home of her grandfather, Charles Rushby, at 31 Asycough Street where Rushby lived with his daughter Mrs Temple. Rumbold asked her aunt if she would look after Harriet while he was away at sea and she agreed. Harriet had stayed with them before, about six months previously. Rumbold paid for her board and lodging there and then.

A fortnight later, on 7 November, Rumbold landed at Grimsby with his crippled vessel and went at about half past seven that evening to 31 Asycough Street. He had a surprise. Charles Rushby told him that Harriet had not stayed there and he hadn't seen her during the last fortnight.

'Have you any idea where she is?' asked Rumbold grimly.

But Rushby hadn't. Rumbold was silent for some time. Then he spoke again.

'I think I might have an idea where she might be.' His face had a set look. 'I shall find her before the night is out.'

The next port of call for Rumbold was a gun-maker's shop at 154 Victoria Street. He was smoking a cigar when he entered and asked the proprietor to show him some revolvers. This was not unusual

Stanley Street, where Henry Rumbold lived, as it is today.

at the time. Many fishermen carried pistols when they went to sea. The shopkeeper showed him some at 5s 6d and 7s 6d but Rumbold asked for one at around 12s. He was shown one at 15s and since the proprietor wouldn't come down in price, Rumbold bought it as well as a box of fifty cartridges.

He then arrived at 12 Emerson's Buildings, the home of Ann Widall, sometimes known as Ann Topliss, or Tet Topliss. Rumbold supplied a bottle of gin and one of Ann's friends brought glasses and drinks were handed round. When he said to Ann, 'Where is she?', she knew them both so well that she didn't have to ask him who he meant.

'I have seen her at the Empire.' (The Empire was a music hall in Victoria Street.)

'Was anyone else present?'

Ann nodded and one of her friends said, 'I've seen her with Mrs Bowdidge and her husband and another man. They were sitting down at the Empire.'

Rumbold asked for the address of Mrs Bowdidge and Ann wrote it down for him. But he didn't have to go there to find Harriet because he later saw both Mrs Bowdidge and Harriet walking together in Cleethorpe Road.

Mrs Bowdidge was the wife of a fisherman and lived at 124 Tunnard Street, the house being between Rutland Street and Park Street. She afterwards described Rumbold's demeanour as being 'very cool' towards them, but he nevertheless went into the Exchange pub (sometimes known as the Barrel) with them where they had a few drinks. They then went on to the Empire, but Rumbold only wanted to stay half an hour, so back they went to the Exchange. It was here that Harriet took Mrs Bowdidge aside and asked her for the key to the house in Tunnard Street. Mrs Bowdidge gave her the back-door key and Harriet left with Rumbold.

Contemporary view of Tunnard Street where Harriet Rushby was murdered.

Mrs Bowdidge later said in court that Harriet had come to her a fortnight before saying that she had nowhere to go and so Mrs Bowdidge took her in and Harriet had been living with her ever since. Mrs Bowdidge left the Exchange after Harriet and Rumbold had gone and was seen on the way home by a young fisherman who lodged with her. He was William Burns and he saw his landlady at the top of Albert Street on her way towards Tunnard Street. He caught up with her and they arrived at the house together.

The door was opened by Harriet and they went into the middle room. Harriet sat on a couch with Rumbold, but they were obviously on bad terms and arguing with each other. Rumbold was complaining that she had been unfaithful to him. Even when he brought out his gin bottle and Harriet poured the drinks, he accused her of winking at young Burns.

'Is he one of your fancy men then?' he asked her.

'Oh no,' replied Burns. 'I hope you don't think it's me, because I'm only a deck chap and I don't think she would be so foolish.'

But Rumbold continued to rail against Harriet, using foul language, and saying that he had £40 which he had been going to spend on her, but now he would not. Harriet hotly denied being unfaithful and Rumbold hit her across the mouth with the back of his hand. Mrs Bowdidge complained to him about his conduct, but he said he was to be the master here. Then Harriet got up from the couch.

'I'm going to get a candle. Then I'm going up to bed.'

But Rumbold stood up and grasped her arm. He swung her round in the direction of the stairs. Then he turned to the others.

Another contemporary view of Tunnard Street.

'Goodnight. If we don't meet again in this world we shall meet in the next.'

They went together up the stairs and into the bedroom at the front of the house. It was afterwards discovered that Harriet had taken off her long skirt and had turned down the covers as if they were preparing to go to bed. But a short time later Burns and Mrs Bowdidge downstairs heard a scream from the bedroom. Mrs Bowdidge rushed up the stairs and when she reached the bedroom door she heard Harriet shout, 'Don't murder me Harry, in my sins!'

Mrs Bowdidge tried the door but it was locked. She banged on the door. 'There are three policemen coming!'

But Rumbold shouted back, 'If anybody comes in here I'll blow their brains out.'

Mrs Bowdidge then heard two shots. She rushed downstairs to William Burns. 'He's shot Harriet!'

She went to the foot of the stairs again and shouted up. 'Oh, Harry! Come downstairs!'

The two of them sat waiting for nearly ten minutes before Rumbold appeared. Burns noticed when Rumbold reached the bottom of the stairs, that he had blood on his hands.

'What have you done, Harry?' quavered Mrs Bowdidge.

Rumbold did not answer her. 'Where's my hat?' he asked. Burns gave it to him.

'Where's the back door?' Neither of them said anything. Rumbold shrugged his shoulders and went out of the front door.

Burns and Mrs Bowdidge rushed upstairs and into the front bedroom. They saw Harriet lying on her back by the fireplace. There was blood on her head and a spreading pool beneath her. Both of them decided that she was dead and they went for a policeman.

Grimsby Town Hall Square in the early 1900s. (David N. Robinson)

They found PC Saunby in Victor Street. He came back with them, saw the body and called for more officers and a doctor. When Dr Brocklesby arrived, he superintended the removal of the body to the mortuary and a post-mortem was carried out. Dr Brocklesby found only one wound, though undoubtedly two shots had been fired. A bullet had entered her skull just below the left ear and was found beneath the scalp above the right ear. The damage to her skull and brain was extensive and Harriet would have died instantly.

Chief Constable Pickersgill was informed of the murder and went to Tunnard Street himself. He examined the body and the room and seeing another large pool of blood nearer the door of the bedroom concluded that the body had been moved. Rumbold said afterwards that he had moved her. The chief constable instigated a search for the fisherman.

Rumbold had gone back to his lodgings after shooting Harriet. It was about half past twelve when he called up to his landlord, Charles Whiting, who was in bed. Whiting threw on some clothes and came downstairs. Rumbold looked dazed and dishevelled and there was blood on his hands.

'Will you take charge of my charts and log books, pack them up and give them to my brother when he lands?'

Whiting and Rumbold had been friends for many years. The shipwright asked him what was the matter and Rumbold said, 'I've killed that girl.' He described looking for her in the evening, buying a revolver and going back to Tunnard Street with her.

'She told me lots of things. Perhaps some were true and some were lies. What she told me made me do what I have done.'

Whiting asked him if he thought that Harriet was dead. 'I think so. I picked her up and kissed her and laid her down again and came away. What shall I do Charley?'

'If I were you, Harry, I would give myself up.'

'Yes. I think that is what I must do.'

About two o'clock that morning, Sergeant Brocksom was on duty in Town Hall Square when Rumbold, who was smoking a cigar, came up to him. Together they went round the corner to the police station and there Rumbold admitted that he was a murderer and gave details of what he had done. He was cautioned by the sergeant and then charged. Rumbold produced the revolver and the box containing the remaining cartridges and claimed that after shooting Harriet he had tried to shoot himself but the gun had jammed. However, when the caps of the cartridges were examined it was found that only the ones which had been fired showed marks. The remaining ones had no marks on them, which made it very unlikely that an attempt had been made to fire them.

The inquest took place on the afternoon of the day following the murder in the old council chamber of the town hall and the jury returned a verdict of wilful murder against Rumbold. The next day he was brought before the magistrates and committed for trial at Lincoln Assizes. His trial began on Wednesday 29 November before Mr Justice Charles. Mr Fordham and Mr Thomas were the prosecutors and Rumbold was defended by Mr Stanger. He tentatively proposed a defence of insanity, but the judge rapidly disposed of that saying that there was no evidence for that at all. Mr Stanger then tried to put some letters in, written by Harriet and also by Rumbold, presumably for some sort of mitigation, but they were also ruled as inadmissible hearsay evidence.

The jury took only eight minutes to return a verdict of guilty and when Rumbold was asked if he had any reason why sentence of death should not be passed on him he said, 'No, sir'. He would prefer death to a life in prison and he had only one request to make and that was for a plentiful supply of cigars and cigarettes before he was executed.

Rumbold retired to his bed in the condemned cell at the Greetwell Road Prison on the night of Monday 18 December. He was awaked early the next morning and taken immediately to a cell connecting with the scaffold, known as the pinioning cell. Here he met and was spoken to by the prison chaplain. At half past eight the chaplain was followed by the Bishop of Lincoln who administered the last rites. At a few minutes to nine o'clock James Billington, the executioner entered the cell with his assistant, William Warbrick. They had arrived at the prison the previous day to test the scaffold and work out the drop, which depended on the weight of the prisoner. Rumbold weighed just over fourteen stones and a drop of five feet was calculated.

At a quarter to nine, six press representatives were admitted to witness the execution and they were conducted to the scaffold, which was a permanent structure in a recess formed from a corridor leading to the men's and women's parts of the prison. It was screened from outside observation by a high wall some twenty feet away. The platform was eleven feet from the ground and level with the corridor and the pinioning room and from the platform hung a tarpaulin so that when the prisoner fell through the trap he would not be visible to the watchers.

At precisely nine o'clock the door to the execution chamber was opened by the chief warder and the procession entered the cell. The chief warder was followed by the prisoner Rumbold, pale of face, dressed in the same suit as he wore at the trial except that his neck was bare and his arms strapped behind him. He was followed by Billington and his assistant, the prison chaplain reading the burial service, the prison governor and the prison medical officer and, finally, more prison officers.

Rumbold was led to the centre of the trap and while Billington stepped to the lever his assistant strapped Rumbold's legs, put a white hood over his head and adjusted the noose under his chin, so that when the trap opened and he fell, the noose would slide round to the back of his neck and jerk his head forward causing dislocation of his neck and instant death. When

Billington pulled the lever Rumbold dropped with a loud thud. His body was left to hang for one hour, and then it was cut down and an inquest held immediately.

In the meantime, as soon as the lever was pulled a black flag was hoisted over the prison and the crowd of 130 people who had gathered outside knew that the execution had taken place.

five

HAYTER AND OSTLER
A Tragic Love Story

The couple trudged hand in hand across the beach, their feet making deep indentations in the wet sand. It was dark but a faint moon above them gave a cold, dim light. They stopped before the water's edge and turned to face each other.

They were respectably dressed, for this was 1922. The man, who was in his forties, was rather short and stout, and had on a grey suit, a brown trench coat and a trilby hat. The woman, much younger, was wearing a blue serge dress trimmed with red needlework and beads, and a blue coat with a blue velvet hat.

They kissed and clung together for a moment before the man pulled away. A few moments later two shots rang out.

They were heard by James Cramm, the groundsman for the Sutton on Sea golf club who lived nearby on Huttoft Bank, a remote, isolated spot two miles south of Sutton on Sea. He put it down to someone shooting rabbits and thought no more about it.

The next morning, Thursday 12 October 1922, he was out sweeping one of the greens. Huttoft Bank rises above the foreshore so that Cramm was able to look down on it. In the distance towards the sea he could see two dark objects separated from each other by a few yards. At that moment he saw a local farmer, Mr J.R. Banks, coming along the road that runs along the top of Huttoft Bank in his horse and trap. He waved to him and together the two went down to the beach to discover the bodies of a man and a young woman which had been washed over by the incoming tide which had since gone out.

PC Frank Osborne of Sutton on Sea was summoned and he reported later that he found the couple lying on their backs on the wet sand. A few yards away he found a double-barrelled shot gun embedded in the sand. The barrels had been shortened, presumably to make it easier to carry in the deep pocket of the trench coat, and in the weapon were two discharged cartridges.

He arranged for the bodies to be taken to a nearby disused cottage, sent a message to his superior in Mablethorpe and later began searching the bodies. On the woman he found a pair of scissors, a small mirror and comb and a little leather purse which was empty of money. The man only had 9d in his pockets, a pair of glasses, a pen knife and a broken gold Masonic ring that he wore on his finger. The woman was wearing a wedding ring.

Police Sergeant Sharman of Mablethorpe tracked the pair down to the Book in Hand Hotel in Mablethorpe. They had registered as Mr and Mrs Hayter of Grimsby, Lincolnshire. Mary Haw, a domestic servant at the hotel said that they had arrived on the night of Wednesday 4 October, saying that they would stay one night and might stay for a week. They had seemed reasonably cheerful and spent most of their time out of doors, except for the last day, the following Wednesday, when they seemed a bit depressed. They went out that evening at about six o'clock saying that they were going to see some friends. But though she waited up for them till eleven o'clock they did not return. They had not paid the bill.

They had left behind two suitcases. In his examination of these, Sergeant Sharman discovered, among a few cheap clothes in one, a sealed packet addressed to the coroner and a letter to Mrs Berry who was the proprietor.

The letter to the coroner read:

Dear Sir,

When you have read the enclosures will you please seal and post them to those they are addressed to. You will then know the reason we have taken this step. I have had nothing but worry and financial difficulties since I was demobbed from the navy. And when I did have a chance the enclosed letters are the result. Neither of us fear what we have determined to do and I am sure it is the only way, as this is the country they said would be fit for heroes to live in: but we are going to try the other.

Tom Hayter.

Contemporary view of Huttoft Bank, looking towards Sutton on Sea, showing the beach on the right and the golf course on the left.

View of Mablethorpe in the 1920s showing the Book in Hand Hotel, the bay windows on the left beyond the garage. (David N. Robinson)

There was also a letter from the woman to her parents in which she said that she had gone away with the man she loved, 'who is now my husband', she wrote. 'When you receive this I shall have passed into the land of beyond with the only man I love.'

A post-mortem was done on the bodies and the pathologist reported that the woman had been shot in the heart. She must have opened her coat to receive the shot since there was no burning on her coat. He estimated that Hayter must have retreated a few steps before he fired at the woman and then he must have turned the gun on himself, since he, too, had received the blast to the chest.

Enquiries had been made by Police Inspector Dawson of Alford who found that Thomas Hayter originally came from Manchester but for some years had been living in Grimsby at 63 Victor Street and working for Messrs A.R. Watson as a motor mechanic. He had married a woman from Aberdeen when he was still in the navy and they had a daughter.

But it seems that Hayter coveted the country life and in December 1920 he and his wife and family moved to North Thoresby, a village stretching between the A16 and what used to be the railway line from Grimsby to Louth, some eight or nine miles south of Grimsby. There he rented a furnished cottage. He made a little money by working as a chauffeur and car maintenance man to a Mr Goulding who lived in the village. Hayter's wife became ill during the birth of her second child and though she was nursed by a neighbour, a Mrs Ostler, the wife of the local shoemaker, she and the baby both died in Grimsby Hospital in February 1921.

Hayter subsequently sent his four-year-old daughter to live with her maternal grandmother in Aberdeen and in April 1922 went to live with the Ostlers. It must have been something of a crush since Albert Ostler, who had lived in the village for forty-two years, and his wife had nine children. Two had died and some had grown up and moved away, but many were still living in the little cottage.

Victor Street as it is today.

One of these was Eva Annie. She was twenty-one and had worked for a time as a domestic servant in the village before moving to Leeds with one of her sisters and working in a factory there. But she suffered from ill health and after working for a time in Grimsby she came back home and had been living there for about a year before the tragedy.

When and how the relationship between Hayter, who was forty-three, and the young girl developed will probably never be known, but it did become obvious to her parents. Albert Ostler took exception to it and told Hayter to leave and the motor mechanic went to lodge with a Mrs Adlard in the village at the beginning of September. He also rented a yard adjoining the New Inn, which is at the end of the village and was in fact next door to the old station at North Thoresby. He used the yard as a garage for car repairs.

He does not appear to have been very popular in the village since he did not seem to do much business and Mrs Adlard said that he was inclined to be sullen when he had had a drink and that she and her husband had decided to ask him to leave when he returned from his last trip away.

Hayter never returned to the Ostler house after he left and Albert Ostler had no idea that his daughter was continuing to see him, although she had told her mother that she would give them a surprise. And indeed, Albert does not appear to have been on bad terms with Hayter for he had a drink with him on the night of 3 October, the day before Hayter and Annie left, but Hayter did not mention that he was going away the next day.

Her parents had no idea that she was leaving with Hayter, since when she left at about 4.30 p.m. on the afternoon of 4 October she said she was going to see some friends. Hayter himself did tell Mrs Adlard on the Sunday before that he would be going away on the following Wednesday

The New Inn, North Thoresby, in the 1920s. (David N. Robinson)

and he left early that morning. He said that he was going to London for a couple of days and would catch a fast train from Grimsby at midday.

A heartbroken Albert Ostler identified the body of his daughter and that of Thomas Hayter. In an interview Mrs Ostler said, 'Annie was such a good girl'. Such is the tragedy of love. But there was a sequel to this tragic story.

Only a few days after the report of the shooting appeared in the newspapers a woman in London reported that she was in fact married to Hayter. Annie Ostler had said in her letter to her parents that she was married to Thomas Hayter, but no record of such a marriage was found and it seems very unlikely that they were. The woman in London claimed that she had married Hayter in London in August 1917 and said that she could produce the marriage certificate to prove her claim. She said that there was one child of the marriage. Hayter had deserted her and she had obtained a maintenance order against him and he had sent her payments; some indeed came from North Thoresby. She also said that she recognised him from the photograph published in the newspapers and could identify him from specific marks on his body.

So was Thomas Hayter a bigamist, conning women into marriage? Or was he a weak character, taking the line of least resistance where his appetites were concerned? Certainly the inquest jury were in doubt as to the true character of the dead man. They brought in a verdict against him of suicide (which was an offence in itself at the time) and murder.

six

CHARLES SMITH
A Lethal Triangle

The 1903/04 season was a frustrating one for Grimsby Town Football Club. At the end of the previous season they had dropped from the first division to the second and were desperate to get back. Yet they were able to finish only sixth in the final table. This failure was in spite of the signing of several new and exciting players, notably Charlie Roberts who went on to captain Manchester United to their first championship and FA Cup wins, as well as a move from their old ground at Abbey Park to the new one at Blundell Park in the summer of 1899.

Mr J.H. Alcock was building a new hotel in Cleethorpes called The Imperial and he had leased some land at the back of the site, to the north and towards the railway, called Blundell Park. Grimsby Town Football Club took over the lease from him, moved some of their stands from Abbey Park and built others, and became – because Blundell Park is just inside the Cleethorpes border – the only club in the football league who never played at home.

Blundell Street (now known as Blundell Avenue) ran alongside the ground from Brereton Avenue to Harrington Street, crossing Grimsby Road about halfway along. In this street a young woman named Eliza Brown lived with her mother and her father who was a fisherman. In the spring of 1904, she married Charles Smith and thus set the fuse of what was to explode into tragedy in the summer of that year.

Charles Henry Smith was twenty-three. He had been a fisherman, but had left the sea since he got married and worked as a fitter for the Great Central Engineering and Ship Repairing Company, popularly known as the Box Company. He had been lodging in Daubney Street. Daubney Street was, and still is, in Cleethorpes but in those days ran parallel to Blundell Street from Harrington Street all the way up to Clee Fields.

Smith had lodged with a Mr and Mrs Prior in Daubney Street. George Wells Prior was a fisherman. His mother, who was separated from her husband, ran an off-license and lived over the premises at 249 Freeman Street, near the cycle club and Hainton Square. George Prior's wife was called Alice and her maiden name was Grundy. She was an orphan and had been brought up by her aunts. One of these women was in Liverpool, where Alice had lived for a time, and the other was in charge of the laundry at Grimsby Hospital. She was described by her mother-in-law as having a quick temper and being quite capable of standing up for herself. Today we would probably call her feisty.

Smith had lodged with the Priors for some years before he began courting Eliza Brown. Theirs was a rather stormy relationship and they had frequent rows. At one stage they broke off their engagement. However, Smith wrote to Eliza; reconciliation was effected and they were married by special licence on Easter Sunday 1904.

Contemporary Daubney Street, the home of Charles Smith.

Smith must have been on very good terms with his landlords for when he married Eliza the Priors vacated their house in Daubney Street and went to live with Mrs Mary Prior in Freeman Street so that the Smiths could move in. The families continued to remain friendly and quite often the Smiths would visit the Priors in Freeman Street and Alice Prior would pop in to Daubney Street.

On the evening of Wednesday 1 June, when the Smiths had been married just eight weeks, Mrs Mary Prior said to her daughter-in-law, 'We haven't seen Eliza and Charlie for some time. Do you think they are all right?'

'Do you want me to go round and see them?'

'Would you? I think that might be a good idea.'

That evening Charlie Smith got home from work at about 5.30 p.m., which was about his usual time. He and his wife had tea and then, according to Eliza, they read the paper together. At about seven o'clock Smith asked his wife if she was going out that evening and she said no. He said that he was going out to meet a man at the Clee Park Hotel, which was on the corner of Grimsby Road and Park Street. He didn't say who the man was or why he was going to meet him. But he was back at about eight o'clock. He came in the back way. Some of the houses in the street were called 'passage houses' since they had a passage running along the side and the back gate opened on to the passage about halfway along it.

It was a fine evening and Smith played with his dog in the back garden and talked to his next-door neighbour over the garden fence. It was a picture of domestic tranquillity, the sort of evening which many couples share and which must have been repeated in houses all over the town that fine summer evening. There was no indication of the terrible events which were to follow.

Smith came in from the garden at about quarter to nine and had a wash.

While he was there Alice Prior arrived. When she came in she said, 'I came to see whether you two were dead or alive. We haven't seen you for three weeks.'

The two women started chatting and Smith came in from the wash house. He sat in his usual armchair with its back to the door.

'Are you going to stay for a bit of supper, Alice?' he said.

'No. I don't think I will. I was thinking of going for a walk.'

'It'll be dark soon. Why don't you stay and have something with us. We haven't seen you for such a long time.'

'Oh, alright, perhaps I will stay.'

'What will you have? Will you have some fish and chips?'

'Yes. I don't mind what I have.'

'Eliza, dear. Would you go and fetch some?' Smith put his hand in his pocket. 'I'll give you some money.'

Eliza put her hat on but didn't bother with a coat as it was a warm evening. The fish shop was Johnson's fish shop on Grimsby Road, just opposite the Clee Park Hotel, so she did not have far to walk. But there were quite a lot of people about for, even in those days, Grimsby Road was a busy thoroughfare. She found that there were two people in front of her at the fish shop so she had to wait a few minutes before she was served.

Looking back on it afterwards, it was hard for her to tell exactly how long she had been out of the house when she returned. It could have been as little as ten minutes; it could have been as long as half an hour.

Freeman Street in the early 1900s where Mrs Prior ran an off-licence. (David N. Robinson)

She came in through the front door, carrying the warm packets of fish and chips wrapped in newspaper. There was silence from the middle room where she had left her husband and Alice Prior, but a curious, acrid smell lingered about the place. She went into the middle room. The gas mantle was still lit. Charlie had lit it before she left. But she could see neither him nor Alice. Then she saw a figure on the floor by the dresser. Its face was turned down towards the floor so she could not see who it was. But it was moaning.

Then she saw that it was Alice. At first she thought that Alice had suddenly been taken ill, but then she saw that there was blood on her head and she appeared to be moving it about and moaning all the while. Eliza moved the table aside so she could get nearer to the prostrate woman. Then she saw that there was another figure on the floor under the table. It was her husband. But he was completely motionless. She bent over him. He, too, had blood on his head.

Eliza dropped the fish and chips and rushed out of the house screaming. Next door there was a small shop run by Mrs Sarah Lackenby and Eliza ran into the shop shouting, 'Charlie and Mrs Prior are dead!' Mrs Lackenby was able to get a garbled version of what Eliza had seen from her and they came out of the shop together. By this time a crowd had gathered, attracted by the shouts and screaming.

A man who was passing across the road came over to Eliza. He was William Mason and having heard her story he went into the house himself, though Eliza did not go with him. He found two people lying on the floor in the middle room. Just inside the door by the dresser was a woman in her outdoor clothes, her feet near the window. She was alive and moaning. Then he saw a man under the table who appeared to be dead. The two bodies were more or less at right angles.

Mason was lodging in Barcroft Street with a police constable from the Lindsey Constabulary, PC Robert Miller. Mason went back to his lodgings and returned with the police officer. PC Miller found that Smith was dead. He was stretched out on the floor with his arms by his side and there was a revolver on the floor between his feet. The policeman picked it up and put it on the mantelpiece: a practice which would be frowned upon today.

A doctor was summoned and Dr William Macdonald, who was acting as a locum for the local doctor, Dr Nixon, arrived at about 9.30 p.m. He determined that Smith was dead and had Mrs Prior lifted up on to a couch. He saw that she had a wound on her left temple an inch from the ear and level with the left eye. There was a great deal of blood on the floor where she had lain. The doctor thought that she was dying, but he sent for a nurse, dressed the wound as well as he could and stayed with the patient for an hour and a half.

By this time, Police Sergeant Chappel and Police Inspector Benjamin Bowles had arrived. The sergeant stayed with Alice Prior and later reported that she died at 3.20 a.m. without having regained consciousness. The police inspector examined the revolver on the chimney piece. It was a six-chambered weapon, still loaded in four chambers. The other two had been discharged but he could not say how recently as there was so little powder on the weapon. He searched the house and found three guns and a number of cartridges. There was also a gun licence taken out by Smith the previous August to cover the possession of a revolver.

He reported later that enquiries had been made at all local gunsmiths but they could not establish where the revolver had been obtained. He was of the opinion, however, that it was perfectly possible for revolvers to be obtained on the fish docks, since most fishermen took guns with them to sea. Smith's father said that his son had been in possession of a revolver in the last six months, but it was not the one found in the house.

The inquest was held at the Clee Park Hotel on the afternoon of Thursday 2 June 1904. The Grimsby county coroner was Mr Richard Mason. Inspector Bowles attended, as did the Deputy Chief Constable. As was usual in those days, the inquest jury was taken to Daubney Street to view the bodies. Then back at the hotel the coroner outlined the case and called several witnesses. Mrs Eliza Smith claimed that her marriage to Charlie Smith was a happy one, but this was disputed by Mrs Mary Prior. She said that Smith had often complained to her that he wished he was not married. Questioned by the coroner she said that she had heard rumours around Daubney Street about a relationship between Smith and her daughter-in-law, but she did not believe them. They were certainly friendly and had been so for a number of years and they sometimes went out together, but she believed that Alice was a good wife to her son. George Prior had sailed on the trawler, the *St. Louis* on the Saturday before the tragedy and was still at sea.

In his summing up, the coroner suggested to the jury, though he admitted that there was no evidence to support it, that there might have been something between Smith and Alice Prior before he married and that later she might have brought claims of some kind on him. They had evidence that she was a fiery-tempered woman and possibly after she had pressed her claims upon him, he had lost his temper and in the heat of passion shot her first and then himself.

What the coroner did not suggest, but in many ways seems equally possible, is that Smith was obsessed with Alice Prior. He got married hoping, possibly, that that would settle the matter, but found that it did not. He was still obsessed with Alice. He got rid of his wife for a short time on that fatal night and then professed his love for Alice. She rejected him. He then felt that life was not worth living and killed her first and then himself.

We shall never know what caused the dreadful events on that warm summer night in Daubney Street, but it did not prevent the jury, after retiring for only twenty minutes, from bringing in their verdict. Charles Henry Smith, they said, had murdered Alice Prior by shooting her in the head and then, being of sound mind, feloniously killed himself with a bullet from the same revolver.

The inquest had lasted just three hours.

seven

GEORGE TURNER
The Errant Wife

'Annie! Annie!'
  'What is it?'
  'Come upstairs, I want to show you something.'
  Grumbling to herself the young girl, Annie Dixon, rolled off the couch she had been sleeping on in the middle room downstairs. She lit a candle and looked at the clock over the mantelpiece. It was ten minutes to seven on the morning of Tuesday 6 September 1904. She thumped her way up the narrow uncarpeted stairs of the little house, 32 Freshney Street, Grimsby, and turned into the bedroom at the front of the house. There were other bedrooms but this was the only one in the house with any furniture in it.
  Inside the bedroom she saw a double bed with three people on it. On the side nearest her she saw the young man who had called to her, George Turner. Next to him lay five-year old Mary Dixon, the illegitimate daughter of her sister Agnes. The child looked to be asleep. Next to her lay Annie's sister, Agnes, George Turner's wife, who also looked as though she was sleeping. But when Annie approached nearer she saw that her sister's face was black and there were livid marks on her neck.
  'She's dead, Annie,' said Turner. 'I've killed her!'
  The young girl turned and clattered down the stairs and out into the quiet street. In those days Freshney Street ran from Corporation Road down to the hospital where it turned into South Parade, which led out on to Alexandra Road. She raced round by the hospital into South Parade, then into Alexandra Road and Flottergate, looking for a policeman. She finally found one in Victoria Street and burst out with her story and the policeman, PC James Urquhart, accompanied her back to Freshney Street.
  When he went up the stairs into the bedroom he found a similar scene to the one Annie Dixon had described. He carefully examined Agnes Turner. She was obviously dead, since she was cold to the touch and there was froth and blood around her mouth and nostrils. She had possibly been strangled. Annie Dixon, who had followed him up, took charge of the young child, who was unharmed, and took her downstairs. Turner himself was lying on the bed groaning.
  'What have you been up to, Turner?'
  The young man turned a bleary eye on the constable. 'I was driven to this. I strangled her.'
  But to PC Urquhart he looked strangely dopey. 'What have you taken?'
  'I've had two ounces of laudanum. The bottle is somewhere about.'

Victoria Street in the early 1900s where Annie Dixon found a policeman. (David N. Robinson)

The constable pulled back the bedclothes and saw a small bottle with a red label lying in the bed. It was marked 'laudanum poison' and underneath this was the inscription, 'W. Barker, pharmaceutical chemist, Clee Park Pharmacy and Victoria Street, Grimsby'. Urquhart called down to Annie and asked her to bring him up some mustard and hot water. He then made a mustard drink which he gave to Turner and walked the young man up and down the room until he was sick. He gave him some more mustard, but Turner looked as though he was fading fast. The constable got him on to the bed and applied artificial respiration. He was sick again and the policeman kept up the artificial respiration until PC Stamp arrived to help him.

A doctor had been called and at about a quarter to nine Dr William Wallace arrived and said that he thought Turner ought to go to hospital. The two policemen managed to get him down the street and round the corner to the hospital and Urquhart stayed with him giving him cups of coffee and walking him up and down. At about 12.30, Turner seemed to be a lot better and the doctors decided that he was out of danger and he was put to bed. According to Urquhart, Turner then began to talk about the case. He was warned that anything he said would be taken down and could be used against him. But he said, 'I deserve to be hung for what I've done. I bought the laudanum in the afternoon intending it to do for us both, but it has not come off. I told her she would not be any good to another man.'

Dr Wallace reported that Agnes Turner, who in life had been a slight, dark and pretty woman, aged twenty-three, had bruises on the left side of her neck consistent with being strangled with the right hand. A post-mortem confirmed this and the state of the liver suggested that she had been a heavy drinker, but there was no trace of laudanum or any other poison in her stomach.

A steam trawler from around 1914. (David N. Robinson)

George Archibald Turner was twenty-four years old. He was also short but with massive shoulders. He was very fair, had a small, sandy moustache and a ruddy complexion. At one time he had been a fisherman, but then he was employed by the Great Central Railway Company, which ran liners to Hamburg, first as a seaman on the SS *Huddersfield* before she was wrecked in the Scheldt and afterwards on the SS *Lincoln*. He left the ships for a period, working as a gateman at the docks, but then went back to sea in the *City of Leeds*, on which he should have sailed on the night of the tragedy.

In the absence of the borough coroner, his deputy, Mr Arthur Mountain, opened the inquest on the afternoon of Wednesday 7 September at the hospital. The first witness was Miss Annie Dixon, sister of the dead woman. She had identified the body in the mortuary and stated that she had been living with her sister and her husband George Turner at 8 Trinity Street, Grimsby until about a fortnight before. Her sister had been married to George Turner for about three years. But on 12 August there had been a furious row between them and Turner had told his wife to clear out. Annie Dixon left that night but her sister stayed on for another week and then went to live at 32 Freshney Street with a fisherman named John Brown, taking her young daughter with her. She was subsequently joined by Annie Dixon.

Brown had gone to sea on the trawler *Pearl* and was expected back the following Thursday. Turner came round to the house in Freshney Street around midday on Monday 5 September. As soon as he came in he caught hold of both Annie and her sister by their necks and held them against the back kitchen door while he said, 'I will do for you both!' Annie freed herself and rushed out of the front door and went to the woman next door to ask her if she would come in and help them, but the woman said she would not interfere between man and wife. When Annie finally returned, Agnes and Turner seemed to have made up after their quarrel. They remained on good terms for the rest of the afternoon and Turner had a meal with them. He said that he was going down to the docks to fetch his clothes from off his ship and returned at about nine o'clock when they had supper together. Annie fetched some beer, which was shared between Turner and Agnes. Then her sister and Turner went upstairs together to the bedroom, Turner carrying their little daughter in his arms.

Later at the inquest there was a certain amount of argument about what transpired afterwards. In Annie Dixon's version she slept downstairs on a couch, but hearing a noise during the night went upstairs where she could hear her sister and Turner talking. She asked if they were all right and they said yes and invited her in. She poked her head in and subsequently went back downstairs to sleep on the couch again, until Turner called to her at a quarter to seven in the morning.

After she had made her statement George Turner, who was present in a very tearful state under the watchful eyes of two police officers, asked to make a statement himself, as he wanted to dispute parts of Annie Dixon's statement. He was advised not to do so as he was not represented by a solicitor and, after a great deal of argument, finally decided not to make a statement.

Evidence was given by PC Urquhart, Dr Wallace and the pharmacist William Barker. The pharmacist said that someone had come into his shop on the afternoon of Monday 5 September and bought a two-ounce bottle of laudanum, saying that it was for a Mrs Williams. He could not identify the buyer as Turner. However, Mrs Williams was called and she said that Turner and his wife had lodged with her a couple of times and she knew him well. He had often fetched laudanum for her from the pharmacy because she had a painful ankle.

This concluded the evidence in the inquest. The coroner's jury retired for about half an hour and then found that the cause of death was that Agnes Turner was strangled by her husband and that he feloniously, wilfully and with malice aforethought did murder his wife. They also congratulated PC Urquhart on rendering first aid to bring the husband round.

George Turner was brought up before the magistrates on Wednesday 14 September. Since this was an important occasion, the chairman of the bench was the mayor, Colonel A. Bannister and the magistrates included Sir George Docherty, the MP for Grimsby. They all wore black ties. The prosecution was in the hands of solicitor John Barker and Turner was defended by Mr H.K. Bloomer. Turner's stepmother, who had come from Plaistow, near London, was in court as was his grandmother. He was wearing a black suit and tie and a black cap which he took off before he bowed to his relatives and friends in court.

The proceedings were virtually a rerun of the inquest, except that since Turner was now defended by Mr Bloomer, the solicitor was able to cross-examine the witnesses and Turner could now make a statement himself if he wished. But when the prosecution had finished its evidence and Mr Barker said that that was the case for the prosecution, the magistrates' clerk read the formal caution and asked Turner if he had anything to say in answer to the charge.

Mr Bloomer rose to his feet. 'The prisoner reserves his defence and does not wish to give evidence on oath.'

'Do you wish to call any witnesses?'

'No. Not here.'

Mr Bloomer then asked the magistrates on behalf of the prisoner if they could see fit to make any allowance for the defence of the prisoner under the Poor Prisoners' Defence Act, which had come into force the previous year. The magistrates' clerk then pointed out that the Act allowed the bench to do so only where there was a defence, a legal defence, but there did not appear to be one in this case. A certain amount of argument took place, but the magistrates stuck to their point that they would not grant any aid and the chairman told Turner that he would be committed for trial at the Lincoln Assizes. Turner was taken back to the cells and Sir George Doughty left the bench to speak to the prisoner's stepmother who was weeping copiously.

The trial took place on Friday 18 November 1904 at the assizes at Lincoln Castle before Mr Justice Bucknill. The prosecution was in the hands of Mr Walker and Mr Moresby White and Turner was defended by Mr Bonsey. Annie Dixon gave her evidence and was severely cross-examined by Mr Bonsey. She had to admit that her sister frequently went out with other men. Soon after they were married, while he was at sea, Agnes sold his furniture and pawned his possessions and went off to Sheffield with another man. Turner went after her, brought her back and forgave her although she did this again. She took up with a fisherman called John Brown and though there were several rows between her and Turner about it she refused to give him up. This was the cause of their argument in August last when he told her to clear out. During much of this evidence, Turner sobbed bitterly.

When the prosecution had concluded their case, Mr Bonsey put Turner in the witness box. The prisoner said that he had been brought up in London up until the age of fourteen when he had gone to sea, where he had spent most of his life. He first met Agnes Dixon in 1901 when her child was eighteen months old and they had lived together until they were able get married. Agnes left him to go with another man in Colchester and again with a man in Sheffield. Each time he persuaded her to come back to him as he was very fond of her. They had frequent rows over her staying out late drinking and associating with other men.

He went to sea on 21 August and returned on the 27th at about four o'clock in the morning to find the house empty and his wife gone. He searched for her but could not find her and had to go back to sea again. He returned home on 3 September and searched for her over the weekend, offering a sovereign to anyone in the pub that Saturday night who could tell him of her whereabouts. He finally found out where she was staying on the Monday and went round to Freshney Street. He did not deny the words Annie Dixon said he used, but denied gripping them round the necks. He was angry because he had received a bill for things Agnes had pawned.

In bed later that night he pleaded with her to give up John Brown and come back to him but she refused. She said that she was quite prepared to live with him in this house until John Brown came back, but then he must move out. But he could come back when Brown had gone to sea again. Today we might view such a suggestion as indulgence, but in the Edwardian era it was an appalling suggestion. A man might do it, indeed it was not uncommon in those days for a man who could afford it, to keep a mistress, but it would never be countenanced for a woman to do the same. And when she said that she loved Brown more than she did Turner he lost his temper and grabbed her by the neck intending to shake her. She suddenly went limp.

To reinforce the accident theory Dr Wallace had already been cross-examined and had admitted that there were cases on record in which death had resulted simply from a sudden compression of the neck and it was possible that a person might die under such circumstances without any struggle.

The judge summed up strongly in Turner's favour calling him kind, generous, industrious, sober and affectionate, whose suffering had been beyond that of many older men. Of the woman, as she was dead, he would say nothing. The jury had to decide, was her death an accident or had Turner deliberately set out to kill his wife?

The jury were out only eight minutes, returning with a verdict of manslaughter and the judge sentenced him to seven years of penal servitude.

eight
WILLIAM HALL
Revenge is not Sweet

It was an incident which could have happened at almost any time, anywhere and in any pub; a drunken customer becoming abusive and being ejected through the front door. But this was a Sunday night, 26 June and the year was 1831. Sundays in those days were strictly set aside for religious observance and though the fishermen of Grimsby often visited pubs on a Sunday, a certain amount of decorum was expected. Today the incident might well have been of trifling consequence but its repercussions that day in 1831 were enormous.

The young hothead was William Hall, twenty-two years of age, and it took two men to get him out of the door. One was the proprietor, George Kempley and the other man was Edward Button. There was obviously no love lost between Hall and Button, because when the young man had been thrown into the street Button looked out of the pub window and bawled, 'Take him to prison, the rascal, for making such a disturbance on a Sunday night'.

But Hall, having been humiliated like that, was not going to give in so easily. He dragged himself to his feet and shook his fist at the bulky figure of the landlord standing in the doorway.

'I'll have my revenge on you!' he shouted. 'If it takes me seven years to do it!'

But Kempley was unimpressed and Hall slunk away. When he had sobered up a little, however, he began to think a bit more rationally. Swearing vengeance on the landlord was, after all, not a very good idea. All it would do would be to get him banned from that particular pub and Kempley might even spread the word around and he might find himself banned from other pubs as well. Better to pocket his pride and try to make his peace with the landlord.

So back Hall went to the pub, intending to apologise. Yet Kempley would have none of it.

'Clear off, you young scoundrel!' he shouted.

'You won't shake hands?'

But Kempley wouldn't, so Hall left again seething with anger. It seems as if the hurt festered during the week. Two witnesses came forward at the trial to say that they had been working on a sloop with Hall during the week and in conversations with him he repeated his threats of getting even with both Kempley and Button.

Another witness said that he saw Hall on the Wednesday sharpening a knife on a stone. Again on Thursday at dusk, he saw him sharpening the same knife – a small clasp knife with a bone handle – on a stone trough in Mrs Dines' yard. Mrs Dines was the proprietor of the Duke of York public house at 238 Burgess Street, which was situated between Fotherby Street and Lower Spring Street.

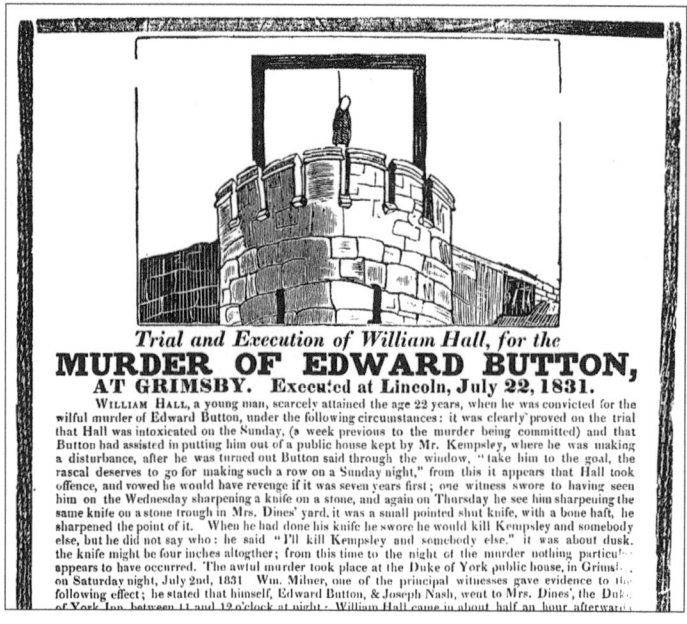

Excerpt from a broadsheet produced at the time of the William Hall murder.

When the first dock was built in Grimsby, around 1800, the East and West Marshes were owned by the Freemen of Grimsby. They soon began to lay out building plots of twelve by thirty yards on the East Marsh and Burgess Street became one of the main streets in the area running from Cleethorpe Road to Pasture Street. It has now largely disappeared, only a small remnant remaining at the southern end leading into Grime Street.

The witness, who watched William Hall sharpening his knife in Mrs Dines' yard, jokingly asked him who the knife was intended for.

'I'll kill Kempley,' muttered Hall, 'and maybe somebody else as well.'

But he did not say who.

It was Saturday night, 2 July, when the next development took place. William Milner a shoemaker of Grimsby, was drinking in the Duke of York pub with Edward Button and Joseph Nash. They were drinking in the parlour, the door of which connected to the street. In those days many pubs were simply houses with a couple of rooms given over to the customers and no proper bar area. It was between eleven and twelve o'clock at night and they had been there about half an hour when William Hall and another man came in. Hall had plainly had quite a lot to drink already.

'Hullo,' said Button who was sitting down, and added aggressively, 'What do you want?'

Hall came over to him and leaned above him so that their faces were almost touching.

'Surely one bully has as much right to be here as another bully?'

At this Button struck Hall in the face, while he was still sitting down. Hall jumped back then walked a few paces to the other side of the room.

'Right! Come on then. I'm ready for you!' He took up a fighting pose.

Button rose from his chair and took off his coat. 'Alright, if that's what you want,' he shouted and charged at the young man. They exchanged several blows then closed and began wrestling with each other. Inevitably they fell to the floor and rolled about, each trying to get on top. They finished up in the open doorway to the kitchen. There was no light in the other room but it

A sloop on the Humber. (Stuart Sizer)

was not absolutely dark since it was early July and there was still some light in the sky outside. To the onlookers, Button appeared to be underneath. He was lying with his head in the parlour doorway and his legs in the kitchen.

Mary Ann Dines, the daughter of the landlady had been sitting in the kitchen. She picked up a candle, lit it and went to look at the struggling figures. She saw that Hall was on top, kneeling with one knee on Button and the other on the ground. Hall looked up and struck the candle out of her hand. Then Button got up and staggered into the kitchen. He tottered a few steps then fell on his back.

Men rushed up, among them William Milner and Joseph Nash, lifted Button and sat him in a chair. He appeared to be grinding his teeth. Then he slumped over and seemed to lose consciousness. He would have fallen out of the chair if they had not held him up. Milner thought that Button had been having a fit until he saw the blood on his hands where they had been holding him. He quickly opened the stricken man's waistcoat and saw a wound in his chest leaking blood.

Mrs Dines who had joined the crowd around Button cried, 'My God! He's been stabbed!'

They looked round for Hall, but he had slipped out of the door. Then he reappeared. Mrs Dines looked at him.

'You've murdered this man with a knife.'

'No, I haven't. I haven't got a knife on me. You can search me if you like.'

'I don't suppose you have now. You've been outside and thrown the knife away.'

'He had a knife with him,' agreed Mary Ann Dines. 'I saw it in his hand, before he knocked the candle out of my hand.'

A doctor was called and he confirmed that Button was dead. He afterwards conducted a post-mortem on the body. He reported that there was a wound on the left side of the chest about 2 inches from the point of the sternum. It could have been caused by a knife passing in

Grimsby Market Place around 1840. (David N. Robinson)

an oblique direction, upwards and inwards, entering between the fifth and sixth ribs, perforating the pericardium and entering the left ventricle of the heart. The knife must have been 3.5 to 4 inches (90 to 103mm) long and about half an inch (12mm) wide. There was no doubt at all that the wound had caused Button's death. After such a wound, the doctor said, a man would die immediately.

The knife was subsequently found outside in the yard and produced in court. Several witnesses at the trial said that it was the same one they had seen Hall sharpening.

William Hall was tried at the summer assizes at Lincoln, which began on 18 July 1831, before Mr Justice Littledale. The prosecution presented their case. Hall had nothing to say in his defence, but two witnesses, Charles Brown and William Nash, were recalled as character witnesses for the young man. They said that they considered him to be a quiet man and they had not heard of his quarrelling or fighting before.

The judge summed up the evidence for the jury. He said that there was no doubt that the prisoner stabbed Edward Button. The question they had to consider was whether Hall, having a grudge against Button, had secreted the deadly weapon, with a predetermined intention of wounding him or taking his life before the fight started, in which case it would be murder; or if finding himself on the point of being overpowered he had drawn it from his pocket and used it in the heat and excitement of the moment; in the latter case they would find him guilty of manslaughter.

The jury retired and after a short consultation came down in favour of the first alternative. They returned with a verdict of guilty of murder.

The judge placed the black cap on his head. He pointed out the premeditated malice in Hall's mind, having on two separate occasions sharpened a knife with the cold and deliberate intent

Lincoln Assize Courts (now the Crown Court).

The roof of Cobb Hall where executions were carried out.

Cobb Hall today.

of using such a weapon against one, if not two, people. He said that the evidence was clear and consistent throughout and that no other verdict would be justified under the circumstances.

'The sentence of the law is that you be taken hence to the place from which you came and from thence to the place of execution and there be hung by the neck until you are dead and that afterwards your body be given to the surgeons for dissection, and may the Lord have mercy on your soul.'

The execution took place on the roof of Cobb Hall at the north-east corner of Lincoln Castle. New gallows were set up there, the so-called new drop, in January 1815 as it provided greater security and a much more impressive spectacle for the viewing population. A total of thirty-eight people were hanged there until 1868 when Parliament passed an Act ending public executions.

Hall's execution was scheduled for Friday 22 July, which was a market day so there would sure to be a great many people in the city to watch the spectacle. In the event, it was harrowing. Hall, who had been relatively calm during the trial and afterwards in prison, collapsed when the time came for the hanging to take place. He had to be half carried to the scaffold, shouting and screaming in terror so that his cries were heard in the cathedral. But eventually it was over and the crowds streamed away.

The sermon which was preached to the condemned man the day before his execution contained the words, 'What hast thou done? The voice of thy brother's blood crieth unto me from the ground.'

nine

SAMUEL SMITH
The Evils of Drink

Samuel Smith was born in 1858. Some eight years before this, a new fishing dock was built in Grimsby. The railway companies Great Northern, Sheffield Manchester and East Lincolnshire tried to attract fishing companies who ran smacks in the south of the country to come and base their vessels at Grimsby. The inducements included cheap rail transport of the fish to London, provision of tugboats to bring the vessels into port and a ready supply of packing cases to carry the fish to the various destinations.

At that time the fishing was mainly for cod. Long, baited lines were used (some of them containing over 6,000 baited hooks) and the smacks had wells filled with sea water to keep the fish alive and fresh until they reached port. Line-fishing smacks had ten or eleven crew members. Smaller numbers were required for trawling smacks, which had usually a skipper, a second and third hand, a cook and a deck boy. But trawling smacks were much less common in that period than line fishing smacks.

In 1857 another fish dock was built and this had floating chests to keep the fish alive until the catch could be sent by rail. However, this process was gradually superseded by preservation of the fish in ice. To start with, local ice was used and then when the demand became too great, ice was shipped in from Norway.

In 1866 the new fish dock was enlarged and by 1870, when Samuel Smith became an apprentice and first went to sea, Grimsby had been virtually taken over by the fishing industry. Lodging houses abounded in the streets near the docks to accommodate apprentices and young, unmarried fishermen. Many businesses were set up to supply ships with provisions, and sail makers and rope makers were present in abundance.

As fishing increased in Grimsby, and by 1889 there were 766 fishing vessels registered at the port, new fishing grounds had to be found. Line fishing for cod was mainly centred on the Faroe Islands, halfway between Scotland and Iceland, and also around Iceland itself. Fishing trips could last three months or more and thus fishermen would be away from their families for long periods. Trawling trips were usually shorter, around ten days, since they fished mainly off the Dogger Bank in the North Sea and off the coast of Holland.

Smack owners with large numbers of vessels tended to operate their ships in fleets. The vessels would keep together and take advantage of any large shoals of fish they could find. The smacks would not come back to port to unload their catches but would transfer them at sea to fast carrier boats, specially constructed to hold large quantities of fish. This could be an extremely dangerous procedure since the smacks would have to disgorge their catches into small boats

Samuel Smith, as pictured in the *Grimsby Evening Telegraph*, December 1904. (*Grimsby Telegraph*)

which would then be rowed across to the carrier vessels. Even a slight swell could make the transfer very hazardous. Fishermen could be injured handling the boxes of fish, or even fall overboard and the boxes themselves could often be lost by slipping through frozen fingers. It was estimated that thirty-five men and boys were lost every year loading or unloading fish at sea.

In addition the fishermen would often be at sea for long periods of time. This could be alleviated to a certain extent by the 'Copter' or barter ships. These often came from Holland or Denmark and at first they would barter clothing and tobacco for skate which was not popular in this country but had a ready sale on the Continent. Then some ships started bringing liquor and tobacco and selling it to fishermen at sea. Since they did not pay duty on the liquor or the tobacco it was a lot cheaper than they could get at home. A bottle of gin cost only 1s. Rum was 18d per bottle and brandy 2s.

Because of the harsh conditions, the deprivation and the ready supply of cheap booze many fishermen became heavy drinkers and even when they were ashore it was common for fishermen to collect their wages after a trip and repair straightaway to a nearby pub. There, they could meet other fishermen, discuss the fishing over a few drinks and also meet prostitutes.

Samuel Henry Smith was forty-five at the time of the murder and liked to be called Harry. He was swarthy, stocky, with a heavy black beard and was called King Coffee because of his dark skin and violent nature. He was also a heavy drinker. When he was ashore he lodged at 4 Fourth Terrace, Hope Street. In those days Hope Street was much longer than it is now and stretched from Bath Street to Wellington Street.

On Tuesday 18 November 1902, Smith collected his money ('down dock' as it was always referred to and still is by many people living in Grimsby) and came back to Hope Street. He went to the home of Lucy Margaret Lingard who lived at 3 Taylor's Terrace, Hope Street. She

All that remains of Hope Street where Sam Smith and Mrs Lingard both lived.

was a thirty-three-year old-married woman with five children but had been living apart from her husband more than a year. She and Smith had been friendly for some time.

When he arrived at her home he found she was having a meal with her father, James Mullins, who was a labourer living in Strand Street. Her thirteen-year-old daughter, Rose, was also there and Smith gave the child some money and told her to fetch him some dinner, probably fish and chips. When she returned, he sent the girl out again for two bottles of stout which he shared with Mrs Lingard and her father. Then Smith had a wash and cleaned himself up.

Some time later there was a knocking on the wall from the next-door house and Mrs Lingard went out to see who it was. She returned to say that Mrs Penny who lived next door wanted her to fetch some beer. Smith put on his coat and together he and Mrs Lingard went to the Gloucester Arms at 113 Albert Street. According to him, they had a couple of drinks there then came back to Mrs Penny's house with some beer and a bottle of gin which they helped her drink. Mrs Lingard went back to the Gloucester Arms and bought more beer and gin.

After this, Smith and Mrs Lingard went to the Smokers Arms Inn in Albion Street, which is still in existence, and had several glasses of whisky. It was a long afternoon and evening that they spent drinking and plainly the couple were having a row, or a series of rows, during their time together. Back at Mrs Lingard's house, young Rose said she saw the couple shouting at each other and Smith hit her mother several times in the face giving her a black eye. It was quite possible that she was becoming tired of Smith and his violent behaviour. Undoubtedly their relationship had been a sexual one. She admitted in the presence of witnesses that she had cohabited with him, which presumably meant that she slept with him, on the 5th, 6th, 7th and 8th of November, sometimes at her house and sometimes at his.

At some point in that long evening of drinking, Smith and Mrs Lingard had become separated and he had gone looking for her. He was plainly in a furious temper for he went to Emma

Garroad's house in Hope Street and shouted, 'Where's the b— cow?' She said she did not know, but he did not believe her and began searching the house. At some point in the search he said that he had something in his pocket for Mrs Lingard and he would hang for her that night.

By about ten o'clock that night things seemed to have simmered down between them. He and Mrs Lingard made up a foursome with John Summerfield, who rented the front room of Mrs Lingard's house, and Naomi Martin, and they went to the Gloucester Arms again.

When they returned to 3 Taylor's Terrace, Smith and Mrs Lingard appeared to Summerfield to be the worse for drink. He and Naomi Martin went to his room and the other two repaired to the back kitchen. But Mrs Lingard said that she was tired and went upstairs to bed. Her daughter Rose, who was still up, later heard her snoring. She also saw Smith lying on the couch in the back room with his eyes closed.

However, after a period Smith roused himself and went upstairs to Mrs Lingard and she came down with him. Together they went into Summerfield's room. It was now nearly midnight. There was obviously not a lot of furniture in the room since Mrs Lingard sat in the corner on an upturned coal bucket and Smith sat on the floor by the fire. He turned to Rose who had come in behind them and told her to get him some supper. She left the room and returned with some bread and meat on a plate and a kitchen knife to cut it.

By this time another row had begun between Smith and Mrs Lingard. Plainly he wanted to go to bed with her and she just as plainly did not want him to. There was a stream of bad language from Smith and loud replies from Mrs Lingard.

'You have a home of your own to go to,' she shouted. 'Go to it. I shall sleep with my children.'

Smith jumped to his feet and wrenched a knife from his trouser pocket.

'What are you going to do?' he bawled, waving the knife about menacingly. 'I don't care whether I live or die!'

The Smokers Arms today, where Samuel Smith and Mrs Lingard went drinking.

All that is left of Albert Street where the Gloucester Arms used to be, another pub frequented by Smith and Mrs Lingard.

Naomi Martin made a rush for the door and left quickly and Summerfield followed her more slowly. Rose crouched down in the corner of the room hoping she would be out of Smith's sight, but she saw him go over to her mother and the knife hand rose and fell several times. Her mother screamed, 'Don't Harry! Don't! I will go with you.'

Smith stepped back and made as if to cut his own throat. He did not go through with it, merely drawing the knife blade across his neck once or twice. Rose could see now that her mother was bleeding profusely from her head and her chest. Smith threw the knife into the fireplace. He was staggering about. Then he began shouting again, picked up the knife and again thrust it at her mother. By this time the poor child had had enough. Screaming and crying herself, she got up and rushed out of the room and into the passage.

She passed Summerfield in the passage. He, hearing the screams of the young girl and her mother and the shouting of Smith, then dashed out of the house himself. He raced along Hope Street to Oxford Street where he came across PC Henry Norton. He blurted out his story to the policeman and then the two quickly went back to Mrs Lingard's house.

She was stretched out on the floor in the corner of the room with blood on her head, face and all over her blouse. Smith was sitting in a chair by the fire.

'I've done it,' he said. 'I hit her four or five times. There is the knife.' He pointed to the fireplace.

PC Norton retrieved the knife and arrested Smith. He sent for a doctor and for further assistance and was subsequently joined by PC Walters who supervised the transfer of Mrs Lingard to the hospital. PC Norton took Smith to the central police station in the town hall where he was charged with unlawfully cutting and wounding Lucy Margaret Lingard with intent to do her grievous bodily harm and stabbing her with a knife. He was lodged in the cells.

Harold Freeth MD house surgeon at Grimsby Hospital later described how Mrs Lingard was brought in at about one o'clock in the morning. He found that she had eleven incised wounds, mainly in the chest and left arm although she did have defence wounds to her left hand. She had lost a lot of blood. Unfortunately at the time, blood transfusions were not common and the prognosis was not good. For a time it looked as if she would rally and hopes for her survival increased but then she relapsed and when, on Saturday 28 November, ten days after the attack, it looked as if the end was near a special court was convened at her bedside. Mr Markham Cook, a justice of the peace presided and also present were the Chief Constable, Detective Superintendent Scott, Dr Freeth and Samuel Smith.

A deposition was taken from Mrs Lingard and she briefly described being stabbed by Smith. He was allowed to question her and it was during this exchange that she admitted to cohabiting with him. Mrs Lingard died at eight o'clock on the following Sunday morning and Smith was subsequently charged with her murder.

He went on trial at Lincoln Assizes on Friday 23 February 1903 before Mr Justice Kennedy. Mr Etherington Smith and Mr Lawrence prosecuted and Smith was defended by Mr Bonner. He could do very little except plead that the accused was very drunk, but the judge pointed out that drunkenness was no excuse for crime and, after only a short absence, the jury brought in a verdict of wilful murder. The judge passed the sentence of death.

On Saturday night, 2 March, a petition for the reprieve of the condemned man was sent to the Home Secretary by Mr J. Whiteley Wilkin of Wilkin & Chapman Solicitors. It contained over 1,000 signatures mainly from fishermen and members of the fishing community. However, a week later a letter was received by Wilkin & Chapman, saying that the Home Secretary could not find sufficient means to advise His Majesty to interfere with the due course of the law. And so, Samuel Henry Smith was hanged at the Greetwell Road Prison in Lincoln on 10 March 1903.

ten

THE RIDLINGTON BROTHERS
Slaughter by Saucepan

In 1909, Victoria Street South, Grimsby, or that part of it between Grime Street and Central Market (what is now Market Street), was lined on one side of the road with a series of small shops. On the right-hand side looking north there was a grocer, a draper and hosier, a greengrocer with Oddfellows' Hall above the shop, a newsagent, a tailor, a tobacconist and a pork butcher among many others. And all of these houses were built back to back. Number 276 Victoria Street South had a house backing on to it that was simply called 'back of 276 Victoria Street'. The latter house had a yard separating it from another house, this one in Burgess Street. Burgess Street in those days ran parallel to Victoria Street all the way up from Pasture Street to Cleethorpe Road. The house in Burgess Street was number 149 and this had a passage running by the side of it. By going along this passage you could reach the yard and so gain access to 'back of 276'. These little passages and courtyards had no lights and on a dark night would have been the perfect place to assault and rob someone… and indeed, to commit a murder. In July 1909 this is just what happened.

In 'back of 276 Victoria Street' lived a man who called himself Alfred Day, although his real name was Alfred Gifford Johnson Cowley. He was twenty-five and a labourer on the docks. He had been living with a woman named Caroline Everitt. She was separated from her husband and came from a large family called the Ridlingtons who always referred to her as 'Carrie'. The Ridlingtons, especially the Ridlington brothers, did not like Day because two years before their younger brother Fred had been living with Caroline and Day, until Day, after a quarrel, had thrown him out. Caroline and Day had been living together for four years, up until Saturday 17 July.

On the morning of that day Caroline said that she saw Alfred talking to some women. It sounds very much as if he was trying to supplant her with another woman and she objected strongly. She saw him later that day, again with another woman and this time her anger erupted into violence. The police were called and she was arrested and charged with shouting, brawling and generally causing a disturbance and put in the police cells.

The next evening, Sunday, five people were drinking together in the Crown and Anchor public house in Freeman Street. They were Thomas Ridlington, a thirty-year-old fisherman, his wife Annie, Alfred Ridlington, who was a twenty-six-year-old fitter's labourer and worked at the new ice works on the docks, and his girlfriend, Lucy Stainton. They all lived at 104 Harold Street. In addition there was John Topple, known as 'Brassie', a friend of the Ridlingtons.

At about nine o'clock, Percy Ridlington, who was two years younger than his brother Alfred, burst in.

Contemporary picture of the town hall, Grimsby. The police court and police station used to be through the last door on the right.

'Hey! Do you know Carrie's been locked up?'
'What for?' asked Alfred.
'Something to do with that fellow, Day.'

It was easy to see that the quick-tempered Alfred was annoyed. He was short and powerfully built in contrast to his brother Percy who was tall and thin. Alfred's face got very red.

'I'll go round and see Alf Day and ask him what it's all about,' he said. 'Then tomorrow I'll go down dock and sub what's owing to me and see if I can bail her out. If it costs me a sovereign I'll get her out.'

But after some discussion it was decided that Thomas and the two women would go and see if they could bail Caroline. They went first to the lock-up in King Edward Street and then on to the town hall. They were unsuccessful. The three then came back up Burgess Street and met Percy Ridlington and Brassie Topple at the corner of Whitgift Street. In those days Whitgift Street led off Burgess Street between numbers 142 and 146 and went down to King Edward Street South.

Alfred and Percy Ridlington and Topple had earlier left the Crown and Anchor and repaired to Chapman's Hotel in Central Market where they had a few drinks, then they too went down Burgess Street.

Lucy said that she, Thomas and his wife Annie met Percy and Topple at the corner of Whitgift Street and Burgess Street. She asked them where Alfred was and Percy said that he had gone home. But it is very unlikely that he had done so. It seems much more likely that he was across the road concealed in the passage leading to 'back of 276'. According to Lucy, the five of them stood about in the street waiting and when asked about it later she admitted that they were waiting for Alfred Day to come down Burgess Street. She said that she had heard the men saying that they were going to give him a good thrashing.

The five waited about twenty minutes until they saw Day coming down the street. Then the two women concealed themselves in a passage in Whitgift Street and Thomas, Percy and Topple went across Burgess Street.

What happened next was described by George Holgeth, the son of Mrs Kelly with whom he lived at 149 Burgess Street. That night he was out in the backyard which was shared with 'back of 276' and although it was dark, he saw two men coming from the direction of Day's house. One was a short, thick-set man and the other was tall and thin. The short man was carrying what looked like a saucepan. Then shortly afterwards he saw him bring it down on the head of another man at the entrance to the passage. The blow made such a clanging noise it was heard several streets away. The man who was struck fell down with his head and shoulders outside the passage. The short man and the tall thin one then began kicking the man on the ground. Another man came across Burgess Street and he too kicked the man in the head. They were then joined by two women, one of whom tried to lift the man on the ground.

The short man said to one of the women, 'Come away.'

'I shan't,' she replied.

'Do you want me to give you one?'

'Alright but I'll give you away.'

They then went away up Whitgift Street.

The saucepan was a small iron one with a lip on one side and the owner, Mrs Kelly, said that it had contained fish and had been out in the yard since the previous day, but somebody must have emptied the fish out to use it as a weapon. She heard the commotion and came out of her front door into Burgess Street to find a crowd of people there including Day, whom she knew. He was staggering about in the road, his head covered in blood and eventually he leaned against her front window.

This was about ten to eleven at night and PC Norton was coming down Whitgift Street towards Burgess Street. He heard the clanging noise and hurried on towards the junction of the two streets. He was passed by a couple hurrying along in the opposite direction. Behind them came another man and then some yards behind him a young woman. The man turned as he passed and called back to the woman, 'Come on!'

As the policeman came out of Whitgift into Burgess Street he saw a crowd of people across the road and a woman told him that a man had been assaulted. He found Day who was bleeding from a cut on the head and asked him what had happened.

The injured man said, 'I was just coming into the passage when a man struck me on the head with a saucepan, knocked me on the floor then kicked me twice on the head.'

PC Norton asked him where he lived.

'Down the passage here.'

He led the officer to his front door, took a key from his pocket and unlocked the door. Going into the house he told the policeman where to find a bowl and towel and the tap and the officer bathed his wound. PC Norton asked him if he knew who had done it and Day said, 'I know the man by sight and I will have it out with him in the morning.'

Several other people had crowded into the house by this time, Mrs Kelly among them, and she asked him if he knew who had attacked him. At first he said he did not, but then after a pause he muttered, 'It's her brothers'.

The policeman told him that he ought to go to hospital, but Day refused, saying, 'It's not as bad as that, constable. I will have a lie down.'

One of the women who had come in was introduced by Day as Mrs Day from Havelock Street. This was a street running across Burgess Street to Victoria Street, between Grime Street and Central Market. Day said that she was his sister-in-law. After some discussion with the policeman, Day finally agreed to go to hospital if Mrs Day would come with him. She agreed and when the officer left Day was putting on his coat. But some time later Mrs Day came running after PC Norton and said that Day was asleep and she couldn't wake him up. He went back to the house and found him lying on the floor unconscious. He called Dr Brace who sent for an ambulance and Day was taken to hospital.

Dr Holden Carson, house surgeon at Grimsby Hospital, said that Day was admitted at about one o'clock on Monday morning. He was unconscious and bleeding from both nostrils, mouth and head. There was a V-shaped lacerated wound on the right side of his head and an abrasion over the right eyebrow which was discoloured and swollen and one on the right temple. His nasal bones were fractured and there was extensive swelling on the right side of his face. He also noted paralysis of the left arm and leg. Day never regained consciousness and died at about a quarter to ten on the evening of the same day.

The post-mortem revealed a semi-circular fracture of the skull. The fracture was depressed and the bone broken into three pieces which had been driven into the brain. Dr Carson considered that the wound could have been caused by a kick or by a blow from a heavy object, such as the saucepan. In his opinion, the cause of death was compression of the brain caused by the blow or blows.

Detective Inspector Baglee took charge of the investigation. Having interviewed witnesses to the assault on Tuesday he went to 104 Harold Street and saw Lucy Stainton and Annie Ridlington who each made statements. Alfred and Percy Ridlington were not there so he went to the new ice factory on Fish Dock Road to see Alfred, but he was not there either. The inspector arranged for a twenty-four-hour watch to be kept on the Harold Street house but neither Alfred nor Percy appeared. The next day he went to 16a King Edward Street, which was the home of the Ridlingtons' father, and found them both there. He arrested them. The next day at an identification parade PC Norton picked out Alfred Ridlington as the man who had passed him in Whitgift Street just before the policeman came upon the disturbance. On the following Tuesday, DI Baglee and Detective Constable Dixon boarded the steam trawler *Victory* in Grimsby Docks and arrested Thomas Ridlington. In addition, DI Baglee arrested Lucy Stainton and Annie Ridlington and charged them both with being concerned with the assault on Alfred Day.

Lucy agreed to co-operate with the police, and charges against her and Annie Ridlington were subsequently dropped. Lucy said that when they were all waiting at the corner of Whitgift Street and Burgess Street, she heard Percy Ridlington say that they were going to give Day a good hiding. Then Percy went across the street to Day's passage, before she and Annie hid in the passage in Whitgift Street and before she heard the sound of the saucepan being wielded. On the way home, while they were in Freeman Street, she heard Alfred say that he had hit Day with the saucepan and that he hoped he had killed the ----. She also said that on the way home, Thomas had admitted that he, too, had had a go at Day and kicked him.

She was criticised by the prisoners at the inquest and the committal proceedings and came under severe cross-examination by the defending counsel, Mr T.D. Lawrence, at the trial. Despite this, she stuck to her story and would not be moved in saying what she had seen and heard.

The trial took place at Lincoln Assizes on Wednesday 3 November 1909. Mr Justice Pickford presided and the prosecution was in the hands of Mr R. Adkins, MP and Mr Blakelock. As regards

The Ridlington Brothers – Slaughter by Saucepan

Harold Street today, where Annie Ridlington was interviewed by DI Baglee.

the evidence, it was by no means an open-and-shut case. There were a number of witnesses to the attack but none of them said they could positively identify the attackers. Whether this was genuine uncertainty or whether they feared reprisals from the Ridlington family will never be known. In fact, the reported words of Day himself (who had named Carrie's brothers as his attackers) and Lucy's evidence, were all that pointed to the Ridlington brothers' guilt.

All three of the Ridlingtons gave evidence. Alfred admitted being in the passage and said he had been attacked by Day. They had fought for the saucepan and somehow Day was hit on the head with it. Alfred claimed to have left immediately afterwards. Percy said that he was never in the passage but saw his brother coming out of it. Thomas also said that he had not seen Day at all that night although he had been in the area.

The case commenced at ten o'clock in the morning and the jury retired at quarter past four that afternoon. They returned after an hour with verdicts of manslaughter against each of the defendants. The judge was plainly surprised with the verdict.

'You stood in great peril,' he told the brothers, 'of being convicted of murder.'

He handed out severe sentences to Alfred and Percy for the lesser charge of manslaughter, giving them fifteen years each. Thomas, since he had not been concerned as much as his brothers, got off comparatively lightly with three years. Even so, Alfred and Percy must have considered themselves very lucky to have avoided the hangman.

eleven

WILLIAM WRIGHT
In Trouble with Mr Wright

Caistor is a small market town nestling high up in a fold of the Wolds, just off the A46 Grimsby to Market Rasen road. It is some twelve miles from Grimsby and is described in the book, *Lincolnshire Villages* as 'a place of steep, narrow, winding lanes, of flights of steps and little passageways and of magnificent views' to the West. It is an attractive Georgian town with a history going back to Roman times, and part of the original Roman wall has been excavated on the southern boundary of the parish church. The name is said to be derived from the Latin word for camp, *castrum*. Before AD100, the Romans established a camp there, probably because of its defensive position, the presence of fresh water springs and its proximity to iron ore mines at Claxby. After the Romans, the Saxons occupied the site. Stories tell of how Hengist, a Saxon general, was given as much land as he could encompass with the hide of an ox, after defeating the Picts and Scots. He cut the skin into very thin strips and was thus able to enclose a substantial area of land and on this he built a castle, which was called by the Saxons *Thuang* or *Thong Castor*.

Caistor men took part in the Lincolnshire Rising which occurred in September and October 1536. It was a reaction to the Acts of Suppression of abbeys and monasteries passed by King Henry VIII. It began in Louth when the population heard that their church would be stripped by the King's soldiers. Armed men took possession of the church and decided to march to Lincoln. They were joined by men from Caistor and Horncastle and by the time they reached Lincoln the force had swelled to 30,000 men.

Sir Edward Madeson from Caistor and others were instructed to ride to London with a letter to the King setting out their grievances. But the King would have none of it and replied rudely, 'How presumptuous then are ye, the rude commons of one shire, and that one of the most brute and beastly of the whole realm, and one of the least experienced, to find fault with your prince'.

The men from Lincolnshire had no real leader and they heard that the King's forces were massing against them at Nottingham, Stamford and Huntingdon. The King threatened to send an army to pillage the county and men began to drift away. By the end of October the rising in Lincolnshire was over. The King promised not to invade the county if prisoners from Caistor, Louth and Horncastle were presented for execution, and over 100 died. Some were executed in Louth and Lincoln and some in London, where they were hung, drawn and quartered. There is an effigy of Sir Edward Madeson in Caistor parish church which commemorates his part in the uprising.

Caistor Parish church.

In 1681 there was disastrous fire and most of the buildings in the town centre were destroyed. They were rebuilt and many of the older buildings in the centre now date from that time. The town centre today still has basically the same pattern as it had in those days and is based on a series of small squares which link up with each other. They are Market Place, Butter Market, Corn Hill and Horsemarket.

From the south-west corner of the Market Place, a steep hill called Plough Hill leads down to Horsemarket. In 1919, Horsemarket tapered down to a narrow lane, before it led on out of town. On one side of Horsemarket there was a row of small cottages which had only four rooms each. One of these small dwellings was near Pigeon Spring, one of the three most important fresh water springs in Caistor at the time, the others being Stott's Well and Syfer Spring. This cottage was occupied by Annie Coulbeck, aged thirty-four years, a single woman who lived alone.

Annie eked out a small living by sewing and she also looked after a neighbour's children during the day. The neighbour, Mrs Plummer, lived only a few doors away. She was expecting Annie to arrive on Wednesday morning, 29 October, and when she had not arrived at the expected time she sent her eldest child, ten-year-old Edith May, round to Annie's cottage.

Edith knocked at the door, but found it open. She pushed it and called 'Annie, Miss Coulbeck', but there was no answer. Edith stepped inside. For a while she could see very little until her eyes became adjusted to the dim light inside the rather cluttered living room. She could not see Annie anywhere and she called again, but once more there was no reply. She moved further into the room and then beyond the table saw a form on the hearthrug by the fireplace. It was Annie. Edith bent to look at her.

She shook her shoulder, 'Annie! Are you all right?'

Contemporary picture of cottages in Horsemarket, Caistor, where Annie Coulbeck lived.

But the lady did not respond. Edith touched her forehead. It was cold.

The young child rushed back home.

'Mother! Annie's laid on the hearthrug and I can't get her to speak."

Fearing that her neighbour had suddenly been taken ill, Mrs Plummer went quickly to Annie Coulbeck's cottage. She, too, felt Annie's forehead and found it too cold to be natural.

'I think she's dead,' she muttered to herself. 'I must get assistance.'

The police were called and they summoned assistance from Dr Alexander Fraser. He examined the body but the dark colouration of the face and the bruises round the neck told their own story. He looked up at the police officer.

'This woman has been strangled! You have a murder on your hands!'

The inquest was held the following Friday at Caistor police station and conducted by the deputy county coroner, Dr T. Anningson, with a jury.

Evidence of identification was given by Mary Ann Bray, the wife of an agricultural labourer, who was living in Horsemarket row. She said that she was a cousin of Annie Coulbeck, who was a cripple and walked with the aid of a stick. Annie was quiet and steady in her habits although she sometimes appeared to be simple-minded; the sort of woman who might be easily influenced. Answering further questions by the deputy coroner she said that last July she had heard that her cousin was associating with a William Wright.

William Wright, a man of thirty-nine years, was a native of Caistor. His father carried on a tailoring business in the town and in his youth Wright had been apprenticed to the trade. However, he had not stuck it for very long and soon after left home and was away for several years. He eventually joined the army and served in South Africa during the Boer War. Then he came back to Caistor and was a familiar figure in the town. At the outbreak of the First World War, he enlisted in the army again and served for two or three years in France. On being demobilised early in 1919 he returned to the town.

Annie Smith was another witness at the inquest. She said that she was a single woman who lived in Nettleton Road. She had known the deceased woman for sixteen or seventeen years. Annie Coulbeck had told her that Wright had promised to marry her. On the previous Tuesday night, the night of the murder, Annie Smith had been walking home at about 9.45 p.m. when Wright overtook her and they walked together for a while. When Annie Smith asked him about Annie Coulbeck, Wright said, 'I'm going to see her'.

Then he added, 'I'm going to see her out of her trouble'.

Answering further questions Annie Smith told the coroner and the inquest jury that she knew that Annie Coulbeck was pregnant.

Dr Alexander Fraser said that, in his opinion, death had occurred seven or eight hours before he saw the body on the Wednesday morning, due to the fact that rigor mortis was well established. He had made a post-mortem examination and found bruises on the woman's face and a band of discoloured blood round the neck. There were also scratches under the right ear. He attributed death to asphyxia and apoplexy, caused by strangulation. Pregnancy, he thought had proceeded to the extent of six or seven months.

Mrs Elizabeth Plummer called Annie Coulbeck a quiet, harmless girl and said that she looked after Mrs Plummer's children while she was out at work. On Tuesday afternoon Wright came to her house and asked to see Annie. Annie then came to see her employer and said that Wright wanted her to go home 'so that he could speak to her for her own good'. Annie went away with

Caistor Police Station, now a private dwelling.

View from South Dale, Caistor, where William Wright's father lived, looking west.

Wright and returned in about an hour. She stayed on at the Plummer house until nine o'clock that night and during that time she told Mrs Plummer that she was pregnant. 'In trouble with Mr Wright,' was how she put it.

Arthur Johnson, a timber feller who lived in Paradise Row was another witness at the inquest. He said that at about 6.40 a.m. on Wednesday, the day the body was discovered, he was passing Annie Coulbeck's home in Horsemarket when he saw William Wright, whom he knew well, coming out of the cottage. He did not speak to Johnson but crossed the road and walked in the direction of his father's house in South Dale, the road off to the left at the end of Horsemarket.

Jim Campey was a chimney sweep. On Tuesday evening he went into the taproom of the Talbot public house and saw William Wright sitting there drinking a pint of beer. He appeared to be very drunk. Campey got into conversation with him and during the half-hour or so that they were together Wright said to him, 'Sweep, three weeks, black cap, rope, hanged by the neck, finish'. But what was particularly damning was that Campey, when questioned by Superintendent Page, reported that he had heard Wright repeat the same words some three weeks before in another pub they were in.

It was not very surprising that when the police were called to Annie Coulbeck's cottage and found her body the first person they wanted to speak with was William Wright. He was widely known to be Annie's lover, and Mrs Plummer would have told them about his visit to Annie the day before her death and the fact that Annie was pregnant by Wright. In those days, this was a very serious matter for an unmarried woman.

Inspector G. Wattam, who was in charge of the case, sent PC Halland to bring in Wright for questioning. When the PC arrived at Wright's house, Wright said, 'I have been looking for you coming, through the window. I quite expected you. Have you heard anything?'

The Talbot Inn today. William Wright had a drink here before going down to Annie Coulbeck's cottage.

The constable replied, 'No. Is anything the matter?'

Wright replied, 'Something worse than the matter.'

He was taken to the police station where he was interviewed by the inspector. He was asked if he had heard the news of Annie Coulbeck's death and he replied that he had not. He admitted however, that he had been with her the previous night.

'Was she alive when you left?' asked the inspector.

Wright took some time before replying. Then he said in a low voice, 'No. We had a few words about a broach. I put out the light and went home.'

Later he made the following statement:

Last night a little after ten o'clock I left the Talbot public house. I had had a lot to drink and I went down to Annie Coulbeck's house. I asked her where she had got the broach she was wearing. She said it was her mother's. I told her I did not think it was. I told her I thought it was one of her fancy men's. She said, 'I am sure it is not, Bill.' I told her I would finish her if she did not tell me whose it was. I strangled her with my hands and left her dead. I put the lamp out and went home.

The inspector was the last witness at the inquest. After he had given Wright's statement as evidence he handed the coroner a paste broach, which he said Wright took from his pocket as he had made his statement. William Wright had elected not to attend the inquest. The jury after a few minutes' deliberation returned a verdict of wilful murder against him and he was committed for trial at the assizes by the coroner.

William Wright pleaded not guilty at the Lincoln Assizes on 2 February 1920, to the charge of murdering Annie Coulbeck. The case was heard before Mr Justice Horridge and he was defended by Mr J.N. Emery who contended that Wright was insane at the time of the murder and therefore not responsible for his actions. His mother had been in an asylum, a sister had had religious mania at the age of seventeen and was now dead and his father's uncle had died in an asylum. In addition to this background, the terrible experiences he had endured as a soldier in the trenches in the war might have affected his mind on the night of the murder.

Yet Mr Emery called no defence witnesses and Colonel F.S. Lambert, surgeon at Lincoln Prison, said that Wright had shown no signs of mental aberration during the time he had been waiting for the trial. The judge pointed out in his summing up that the lucid confession he had made the day after the murder showed that he was aware of what he had done, although why he had done it was a mystery known only to him.

However, those who read this account will be aware that Wright was by no means the first man, nor would he be the last, to find that once he had had his pleasure from a woman there could sometimes be less than pleasant consequences. And he was not the first or the last to discover that the inconvenience of a child born out of wedlock could be eliminated by getting rid of the mother.

To the murder charge, the jury had no difficulty in returning a verdict of guilty and Wright was duly sentenced to death. An appeal was unsuccessful and he was hanged by Thomas Pierrepoint and his assistant William Willis at Greetwell Road Prison on 10 March 1920.

twelve

NORAH WALKER
The Cup that Kills

In 1811 there were three small villages lying on the Lincolnshire coast, a few miles south of Grimsby and Cleethorpes: Mablethorpe in the north, Trusthorpe in the middle and Sutton on Sea in the south, though at the time it was called Sutton Le Marsh. The population of Mablethorpe at the time was 204, Trusthorpe 196 and Sutton 110 and the centres of the villages were no more than a mile from each other. Each of them lay behind extensive sand dunes, some between twenty and fifty feet high. Since the dunes lay at the landward edge of sandy beaches, the three villages became popular holiday destinations in the late eighteenth century. They remain so today.

Accommodation in the resorts in the summertime was, as it is today, often at a premium. Dr George Clayton Tennyson, father of Alfred Lord Tennyson, used to take his family regularly to the area. In a letter written in 1813 from Mablethorpe he says, 'I immediately began to make a more diligent enquiry with respect to lodgings [...] but to no avail. Every pot-bellied grocer and dirty linen draper bespeaks his lodgings from year to year and they are therefore pre-engaged throughout the year [...] There are no lodgings to be had at Sutton – every dirty cottage runs over. At Trusthorpe [...] every miserable shed is occupied [...] as for the inns you cannot be at all decently accommodated in them'.

Up until the coming of the railways, the villages were the venues only for the wealthy and well-to-do of nearby Lincolnshire. But the railways opened up the catchment area to the towns of the Midlands and eventually to the South East. Thus, day trips to the Lincolnshire coast for the not so wealthy became possible. Tents could be pitched on the sands during the Edwardian period and some families would spend weeks during the summer camped out on the beach.

In later years there were plenty of amusements on the sands: boat trips and stalls selling all manner of toys and fancy goods, swing-boats and a helter-skelter, concert parties and photographers who could record your holiday. Yet there were distinct differences between the three villages. Mablethorpe became far more popular, having many more amusements and therefore grew larger than the other two. Trusthorpe remained largely rural. It did not even have a station although the railway line joining the other two ran through it. Sutton claimed to be more select and catered for an older type of holiday maker and it also became a popular retirement town.

Mablethorpe had a steadily rising number of trippers: 92,000 in 1906, rising to a maximum of 166,000 in 1936 and at the August bank holiday weekend the station would be packed with people. The Midland towns often shut down their factories for a week during the annual summer holiday to allow workers to visit the coast.

A view of Mablethorpe beach in the 1920s. (Norman Cawkwell)

The tobacco factory of J. Players & Son in Nottingham closed for a week in 1922 from Friday 14 July and two girls who worked there left on the evening train to Mablethorpe. One was Beatrice Simpson, usually known as 'Beatie', who was nineteen and lived at 5 Walter's Row, High Street, Old Basford, Nottingham, and the other was Norah Walker who was also nineteen and lived in lodgings in Old Basford.

Beatie lived with her father, Joseph Simpson, who worked at the gas works. She had worked at Players since she was thirteen-and-a-half and now worked as a tobacco stripper in the leaf department, earning 49s a week and receiving an annual bonus of £17. She was said to be a quiet, reserved young woman, but prone to fits of depression, particularly since her mother had become an invalid and was now living in Plumstead, near London.

Although she was lodging in Old Basford, Nora's home had always been in Mablethorpe. Her father, Charles Walker, was a blacksmith and had a shop in the town. He had seven children and Norah was the youngest. Her mother had died some years before and when she left school she stayed at home to look after her father until he married again. Then after a couple of jobs in Mablethorpe and Sutton she moved to Nottingham and went to work at the Players factory. She had worked in the same department as Beatie for a couple of years and the two had become firm friends.

Norah's father owned a house in Gibraltar Road, Mablethorpe, close to where he had his shop. He let the house to Harry and Rose Castle but kept a bedroom and a sitting room at the front for holiday guests. And it was this accommodation which Beatie Simpson and Norah Walker were due to share for the week of their holiday.

Gibraltar Road today, much changed from when Norah Walker and Beatie Simpson stayed there, although the sea bank can still be seen.

Beatie's parents received four letters from her during her holiday. They were all cheerful and emphasised that she was enjoying herself, although the weather perhaps could have been better. Winifred Mallison, a friend and work mate of the two girls, received a post card from Norah on 18 July saying, 'Lovely weather for ducks', but which continued, 'We are as happy as gay birds'.

Yet these cheerful expressions belied the undercurrents which were to result in awful tragedy. The first signs that all was not quite normal came earlier, before the girls went on holiday. It sounded innocent enough but Norah mentioned to Winifred Mallison that she would have preferred a fortnight instead of the week they were allowed off. They were both due to start again on Monday 24 July but neither turned up for work that day. During the following week they both went to see Norah's married sister, Ethel Dales, who lived in Louth. They were both full of fun and laughter and explained that they had first gone to Beesby, a mile or so off the road from Mablethorpe to Louth and there called on a friend of Norah's who was named Tom. He must have been a chauffeur or the son of wealthy parents for he drove the two girls on to Louth in Major Jackson's big Humber car, known as the Silver Queen. Not only that but they dressed up in the major's wife's fur coat and his expensive coat lined with fur as well.

They arrived at Ethel Dale's house at about 1.50 p.m. and caught the evening train back to Mablethorpe. Ethel asked them about being late going back to Nottingham, but neither seemed concerned. She asked them if they would get the sack when they returned. Beatie said, 'No, but we shall get a good talking to'. She also asked them if they had enough money and Beatie said 'Plenty'.

Louth Station in the early 1900s, where Norah Walker and Beatie Simpson caught a train back to Mablethorpe. (Norman Cawkwell)

They did not go back that Saturday, or the following one. But on the Friday night before the last Saturday, Friday 4 August, Harry Castle heard them go upstairs to their room. When they didn't come down, he asked his wife to go up and ask them if they had finished in the front room they used as a sitting room, since the light was still on. She went up and came back with the information that they were coming down to use the room shortly. They did so and he didn't hear them go up finally until after twelve o'clock at night.

The next morning at about five o'clock, he heard them go out. He assumed that they were going for an early morning swim as they sometimes did and indeed, their next-door neighbour, Mrs Elizabeth Graves was just getting up when she saw from her bedroom window the two girls returning across the sand hills. Gibraltar Road lies just behind the sand hills.

At between 10.15 and 10.30 that morning, Harry Castle sent his wife up again to the girls' bedroom. He was expecting some more guests later that day to occupy the rooms which the girls currently had and he wanted to see whether they had gone yet so that he and his wife could clean the rooms.

Mrs Castle came down and reported, 'I've knocked twice and called twice but I can't get any answer, so they must have gone, though I didn't hear them. That front room needs tidying up too. You'd better have a look at it.'

So Mr Castle went into the front room.

He drew back the curtains and noticed a small pile of coins on the table. On the mantle piece there were three letters. One was sealed and addressed to Winifred Mallison. Another which was

Mablethorpe Station in the 1920s. (Norman Cawkwell)

Another 1920s view of Mablethorpe beach showing the sand dunes. (David N. Robinson)

not sealed was addressed to Mr Walker. Castle opened it and read, 'Dear Dad – This is the end of things…'

He read no further, but rushed round to Charles Walker's shop waving the letter. When he had finished reading it, Walker asked, 'Have you checked their room?'

'No,' said Castle.

'Come on then.'

The two men hurried back to the house on Gibraltar Road and went up the stairs quickly. They flung open the bedroom door and were assailed by pungent, disinfectant fumes and the acrid smell of vomit. The two girls were lying, apparently unconscious on the bed.

'I saw an empty bottle of Lysol downstairs in the front room,' said Castle.

'I'll go for the doctor. You see if you can get some hot salt water down them.'

Harry Castle told his wife to make up some hot salt water while he went next door to summon assistance. He returned with Mrs Graves and another neighbour, Mrs Hunter, and the two ladies attempted to force some liquid into the mouth of Beatie Simpson. They found it very difficult as while she appeared to be unconscious her teeth were tightly clenched. He and his wife had more success with Norah Walker. They managed to get some of the salt solution into her mouth and held her up so that it would go down and she might be sick.

Dr Colin Iredale, who had a practice in Mablethorpe, had been alerted by Walker and soon arrived on his bicycle. He also made strong efforts to revive the two girls but in the case of Beatie he was unsuccessful and she died at just after twelve o'clock that morning. Her mouth was very badly burned by some corrosive fluid. He was shown the bottle marked 'Lysol' and reported afterwards to the coroner that it normally contained cresol derivatives of coal and caustic potash. He said that, had the eight-ounce bottle been full and its contents taken by the two girls, the dose would be enough to kill them both. Later, to confirm his suspicions, two empty cups, smelling strongly of Lysol, were found in the bedroom.

Norah, who was revived, was taken eventually to the local hospital and began to make a slow recovery. She was not well enough to attend the opening of the inquest into the death of her friend, but on Sunday 13 August she was visited by Inspector Dawson who was stationed at Alford. She was, at that time, still in the house occupied by Harry Castle but she had with her her father, her sister Ada and her brother William. After she had been cautioned, she made the following statement:

Yes, we agreed to die together. We had stayed away too long and were afraid to go back to our work. Beatie went to drown herself but the tide was not done coming in. I waited a minute or two and then went and touched her. She said – 'The tide will wash me in again.' So we came back home. Beatie went out again, but she soon came back again and said – 'A man who works with dad was on the bank watching.' So we both sat up in bed and drank it. We both drank at the same time. We decided some time before to do it together.

This statement was read out at the resumed inquest held at the Mablethorpe Sanatorium on Wednesday 16 August. Norah was present but she elected not to give evidence. One of the letters which the girls had left behind was also read. It was from Beatie to her mother.

Dear Mam and all,

Please forgive me if I am causing you trouble. You've wondered why we stopped three weeks. Well I will tell you. We knew this would be the end of all. Give my love to all and I've thought about everyone

> POISONING TRAGEDY AT MABLETHORPE.
>
> TWO NOTTINGHAM GIRLS FOUND UNCONSCIOUS IN BED.
>
> ONE DEAD, THE OTHER RECOVERING.
>
> An awful tragedy was revealed at Mablethorpe on Saturday morning, when two girl visitors—Beatie Simpson, 20, and Norah Walker, 19, both of Nottingham, were found unconscious in bed from the effects of poisoning by a disinfectant. Simpson died within an hour of being found without regaining consciousness, but Walker is expected to recover. An empty bottle, which had contained lysol, was found in a room downstairs, together with letters, presumed to be from the two girls, one of which was read at the inquest. In the bedroom there were two cups which had also contained the deadly disinfectant. The Louth District Coroner (H. Sharpley, Esq.) was informed of the affair and he held an enquiry, with the assistance of a jury, into the circumstances surrounding the case, at the Convalescent Home on Tuesday. After hearing the evidence the enquiry was adjourned to Wednesday to enable the other girl, Norah Walker, to give evidence, if she so desired.
>
> Miss Walker's home is at Mablethorpe, but she had been living at Nottingham for the last two years, where she had been working with the deceased in Messrs. J. Player & Sons' tobacco factory.

Excerpt from *Louth and North Lincolnshire Advertiser* for Saturday 12 August 1922. (*The Louth Leader*)

of them in their turns today, but please believe me Mam neither of us are in any kind of trouble. You will no doubt wonder why we've done this, but no one will ever know that, only Norah and I. So goodbye, Mam and all love,

Beatie and Norah.

The coroner explained to the jury that, as the law stood at the time, if two persons agreed to commit suicide together and did so and only one survived then the survivor was held responsible for the other's death. The jury had to find the cause of the death of Beatie Simpson and say, if they could, who was responsible for that death. The jury took only a quarter of an hour to decide that the deceased had died by taking poison and the survivor had agreed with her that they would die together.

'Do you realise that the survivor is guilty of murder?' asked the coroner.

'Yes, we realise that, sir,' replied the jury foreman.

The next day at Alford police court Norah Walker was charged with attempting suicide by taking poison, which at the time was also a serious offence. She was then remanded until 24 August, when at the same court she was charged with the murder of Beatrice Simpson. A pathetic and forlorn figure, she sat in the dock for over five hours listening to the evidence against her. Her sister was allowed to sit beside her in the dock and her father sat not very far away. For most of the time she bore up bravely, sometimes seeming a little bewildered by all that was a going on around her. At other times, her hands clutched convulsively at the rail of the dock. But when Sergeant Taylor of the Mablethorpe police went into the box to describe what he had seen and heard after being called to the house in Gibraltar Road by Harry Castle on the day that Beatie died, Norah began to cry.

When the sergeant repeated the words that Norah had said to him – 'I know Beatie is dead and I want to die' – she broke down completely and had to be carried, weeping piteously from the dock. She returned later when she had composed herself but she was by now exhausted and simply waiting for the end. It wasn't long in coming. The magistrates committed her for trial at the Lincoln Assizes on the charges of murdering her friend Beatrice Simpson and attempting to commit suicide herself.

Her solicitor made an eloquent appeal for bail, pointing out that she was in a poor state of health and that the Church Army would be prepared to receive her into a home until the time came for her trial but bail was refused.

The trial opened on Tuesday 31 October at Lincoln Assizes before Mr Justice Lush. Mr O. Sullivan led for the Crown and Norah was defended by Mr P.E. Sandilands. Norah was wearing a dark green hat and a blue overcoat. She pleaded not guilty to the charge of murder, which was a hanging offence in those days, but guilty to the charge of attempted suicide.

Mr Justice Lush felt that the charge of murder should be dropped. He said he felt that the law, stating that whenever two people attempted suicide together and one survived they were guilty of murder, needed revising. The reasoning behind it, he suggested, was that once they have entered into a suicide pact, each individual becomes guilty of inciting the other. However, in this case it was Beatrice who was determined to end her own life, as shown by her letters and by the fact that she attempted to drown herself. Furthermore, it was she who had influenced Norah to attempt suicide. Under those circumstances, he did not feel that a jury would convict her of murder. The jury then brought in a verdict of not guilty without retiring.

On the charge of attempting to commit suicide to which she had pleaded guilty, he felt that he could be lenient. She came from a good family and had supported her father when her mother died. Her employers, Messrs Player & Son thought so highly of her that they were prepared to take her back and had sent Dr Tinsley Lindley to give the court any assistance they could. On the other hand he must pass a sentence to show others that they must not do things like that. Accordingly, he sentenced her to one month's imprisonment. Since she had already been in prison for this time, she was released immediately and walked free.

thirteen

DANIEL REVELL
Act of Murder

In August 1949 Edna Curtis was thirty-eight years old. She had been born in Oldham and came from a family much associated with the music halls. Her father called himself a *siffleur*, in other words, a whistler who could imitate birds and animals and was billed as the Great Shawlene. As a child, his daughter, Edna often went on the stage herself both as a singer and dancer. Later she married a man called Chris Sands who was a trick cyclist and toured the music halls and clubs with him in the North and Midlands area. In 1935 she was singing in a Cleethorpes hotel when she was heard by Roy Curtis, himself a music hall performer who had just come back from a tour of the United States. He recognised that, with her bubbly personality and good voice, she would make a good comedienne in the style of Nellie Wallace, a very famous star of the 1920s, and he suggested to her that they team up as a double act. She agreed and together they worked out some comedy routines. After months of rehearsal they were billed as 'Sands and Curtis' and appeared in Leeds, Sheffield, Leicester, Nottingham, Birmingham and many other cities. They were moderately successful, but audiences were and still are notoriously fickle; styles of comedy change after a period of time and their popularity eventually declined. After war service they returned to Cleethorpes in 1946 and concentrated on bookings in the Grimsby and Scunthorpe areas. Their last booking was in Scunthorpe in February 1949.

By August of that year Edna was working from Monday to Friday at Cleethorpes Laundry, which in those days took in laundry not only from the local area but also from many RAF stations in Lincolnshire. At the weekends during the summer she worked as an attendant at Wonderland. Roy ran a bubble and lucky dip stall on Cleethorpes beach for a Mr Ron Wilkinson who owned the Arcadia Amusements Company, and they both lodged with Mrs Elizabeth Fraser at 37 Neptune Street, Cleethorpes.

About 9.30 a.m. on Friday 19 August, Roy said to Edna, 'Aren't you going to work today?'

'No. I think I'll have a day off.'

She and Mrs Fraser went shopping in the morning at the Freeman Street Market. They stopped off for a drink at the Excelsior Club, carried on shopping then went to the Comrades Club for another. Mrs Fraser said that they shared several bottles of beer in the two clubs. Then they went home by taxi. Edna ordered a taxi to pick her up again at half past five and went out drinking again, this time on her own.

Both Roy and Mrs Fraser later agreed that Edna was a heavy drinker and Mrs Fraser also said that Edna made friends with strangers easily, especially when she was drinking. About six o'clock that evening she was in the A1 Club in Duke Street when she noticed a couple of fishermen.

Contemporary view of Neptune Street where Edna Curtis lived.

One of them, Thomas Lee, afterwards said that he noticed a woman in a flowered skirt and white top sitting near them. She was wearing glasses fitted with thick lenses and he had never seen her before. He and his friend Danny Revell had also been drinking that day. They had started that morning at about half past eleven at the Lincoln Arms. Then they went on to the Alexandra Club in Cleethorpe Road and finished up at the A1 Club. There Revell went over to speak to some cousins of his and while he was away Lee noticed the woman in the thick spectacles sitting nearby.

Revell came back eventually and said to Lee, 'We'll go for a drink somewhere else'.

The woman leaned across and said, 'I've got a taxi coming; do you want to share it?'

Revell looked at Lee, who did not seem all that keen, but Revell said, 'Sure, we'll all go together'.

When the taxi arrived the three got in it and Revell suggested going to a pub in Freeman Street known as 'Miles'. They had three drinks there then Revell, who did not seem to like staying in one place for long, suggested they move on. Edna agreed and they went on to the Lincoln Arms. They arrived at about half past seven and stayed till about quarter past eight when Revell wanted to move on again.

This time Lee demurred. Whether it was because he felt he had done enough drinking for the day – certainly, the other two were described as being quite drunk at the time – or because he thought that Revell, now he had a woman with him didn't want him around, is not certain. Whatever the reason, Lee stayed behind while the other two went on to the Yarborough Hotel. They went into the lounge and the waitress there, Mrs Ivy Weir, served them with a bottle of beer each. However, she kept a careful eye on them for they were obviously very drunk and when Revell called for more drinks she refused to serve them. They left in high dudgeon and together staggered up Brighowgate to Bargate and the Wheatsheaf Hotel. There, Mrs Lillian Braithwaite, who was a barmaid, seeing the two staggering about refused to serve them. It was then about 8.45 p.m.

The Yarborough Hotel where Edna Curtis and Daniel Revell had a drink. (David N. Robinson)

A little before this, a Grimsby Corporation bus left Town Hall Street to go to Humberston, just south of Cleethorpes. When it reached the Wheatsheaf stop five people got on. The conductress, Miss Annie Coote, particularly noticed Revell and Edna because they were very drunk, but somehow managed to get upstairs. They had been seen waiting for the bus by a policeman who noticed that they seemed very unsteady leaning against a fence.

When the bus reached the terminus, which was the junction of North Sea Lane, Church Avenue (now Church Lane) and Grimsby Road (now Humberston Road), the pair came clattering down the stairs. Revell got off first, but Edna stayed on the platform. 'Let's stay on and go back,' she said.

'No,' replied Revell.

Edna turned to the conductress. 'What time does the bus go back?'

'9.25.'

'What time is it now?'

The conductress shrugged her shoulders. 'It's 9.20 now. We just turn round here and go back. You'll have to get off now. But you can get back on when we've turned round.'

Edna seemed reluctant to leave the bus, but Revell put out his hand to take her arm and assist her off the bus and together they walked off along the road towards Grimsby.

When Edna had not returned home by half past two the next morning, Roy Curtis realised that something was wrong and went to the police. It was not until he was out with his stall on Cleethorpes beach later that morning that the police approached him to say that a woman's body had been found in a field at Humberston, and to ask if he would go to identify it. The body turned out to be Edna's. In fact, the Cleethorpes police knew all about this long before she had been officially identified and had a man in custody for the crime.

The Wheatsheaf Hotel today where Daniel Revell and Edna Curtis were refused a drink.

It was about quarter to eleven on Friday night when a Cleethorpes bus was stopped by a man near Church Lane, Humberston. The conductress, Mrs Lillian Wilcox, said that he got on the bus and ran upstairs. She did not like the look of him. He was dirty and dishevelled, the flies of his trousers were open and he had dark stains on his knees, which could have been blood. He was carrying a brown and red shopping basket and he smelt strongly of drink. When they got to the terminus all the other passengers got off, but the man remained upstairs. She went up and found him sitting with his head in his hands.

'You'll have to get off now. This is as far as we go.'

'Take me to a policeman. I've done something awful.'

Mrs Wilcox took him by the arm and shook him. She was convinced that he was so drunk that he did not know what he was saying. 'You can't stay here. You'll have to get off.'

'I've just killed a woman.'

The conductress jumped back in alarm. 'Where?'

The man (afterwards identified as Danny Revell) jerked his thumb over his shoulder. 'In a field back there.'

Mrs Wilcox didn't know whether to believe him or not. She went downstairs and consulted the driver. They decided that they would take no chances. While the driver stayed with the bus to keep an eye on Revell, the conductress phoned the police.

Sergeant Crowe of the Cleethorpes police took the call at about ten to eleven that night. He told Mrs Wilcox to proceed with her journey and he would meet the bus when it reached Cleethorpes market place. In the meantime he got in touch with his superiors and when the bus arrived at the market place, with Revell as the only passenger, it was met by three police officers, Inspector Milbourn, Inspector Rose and Sergeant Crowe.

Inspector Milbourn said to Revell, 'What is the matter?'

'I have killed a woman. This is her bag. Take me and I will show you where she is.'

The three officers looked at each other. Then they put Revell in Inspector Milbourn's car and they all drove off towards Humberston. On the journey, Revell was very talkative.

'The Lord told me to do it,' he said. 'She had a beautiful body. They called her Edna. I met her at the A1 Club. We had a lot to drink.'

Inspector Rose asked him, 'How did you kill her?'

'I know how to do it – with my hands.'

But when they got to Humberston, Revell in his fuddled state could not remember where he had killed Edna Curtis. It was dark and they trailed up and down the roads, but were unable to find her. The police officers took him back to Cleethorpes police station and resumed the search without Revell at five o'clock when it was light. They were not successful this time either. So, at 7.30 a.m. they hauled Revell out of bed and continued the search with him. This time after a few hours sleep his memory was better and eventually he pointed to an iron fence surrounding a field at the junction of Grimsby Road and North Sea Lane.

'That's it. She's in there. I killed her on the grass verge, pushed her body over the fence and dragged her into the field.'

Sergeant Crowe scaled the fence and forty feet into the field discovered the partly clothed body of Edna Curtis lying in the long grass. Revell was taken back to Cleethorpes, arrangements were made to secure the crime scene and a search was made of the surrounding area. The local police doctor, Dr Brown, was called and he examined the body. He estimated that the death had taken place approximately twelve hours previously which would have put the time of death at between ten o'clock and midnight the previous day. This was confirmed by the Home Office Pathologist, Dr Fulton, who arrived from Peterborough later in the day and conducted an autopsy. He said that in his opinion the cause of death was manual strangulation. Considerable violence had been used to inflict the injuries to the neck and there were other injuries which had been caused before death. He could find no evidence of recent sexual activity.

George Daniel Revell, whose age was given as forty and whose address was the Family Bungalow, Snettisham, King's Lynn, was charged with murder, brought before magistrates on 16 September and committed for trial at Lincoln Assizes. But on 4 November application was made for the murder trial to be transferred to the Nottingham Assizes due to the illness of an essential defence witness and the trial finally began on Wednesday 23 November at Nottingham. Revell, who was wearing a blue suit, a khaki shirt and a green, figured tie, was defended by Mr W.A. Fearnley-Whittingstall KC and Mr Malcolm Milne, instructed by Mr Sidney Harmston of Messrs John Barker, solicitors of Grimsby. The prosecution was in the hands of Mr R.E. Manningham-Buller, irreverently known to his contemporaries as 'Mr Bullying Manner' because of his aggressive style of cross-examination.

He brought forward a surprise witness, a woman who had seen a man on the night of the murder kneeling over a woman who was lying on the ground on the verge along the Grimsby road, though she could not identify Revell as the man. However, there was little doubt that Revell had strangled Edna Curtis, as the judge, Mr Justice Jones, pointed out in his summing up. The only defence which could save him from the rope was that of insanity.

Today's busy junction in Humberston. Church Lane is off to the left and Humberston Road is straight on. The murder was committed near the area of trees in the middle of the picture.

Mr Fearnley-Whittingstall produced Revell's brother, Leonard, who lived in Boston. Leonard said that Revell, who was born at Boston, was the sixth of eleven children and when he left school became a fisherman, working chiefly from Grimsby. He was married at the age of twenty-one and had four children. When one of his children, a three-year-old girl, died his whole personality seemed to change. He would spend long periods standing by the grave saying that he should be there instead of his daughter and he took to reading the Bible. He became intensely religious and was an ardent member of the Scripture Union and always carried a Bible with him. He was known to drink heavily, but had never been know to be violent during the drinking bouts. Since he was nineteen years old, Revell had tried to commit suicide seven or eight times and there was a history of mental trouble in the family. A cousin had died in Lincoln Asylum.

Dr Duncan MacMillan reported that Revell had been certified insane at Maperley Mental Hospital in March 1941, but the next day he had been alright. On cross-examination he said that the circumstances of recovery were no guarantee against a recurrence of the condition.

Dr A.A. Radcliffe, a psychiatrist, said, 'It is my opinion that at the time of the act this man was suffering from a disease of the kind induced by alcohol of such a nature that he would not know what he had doing and he would not know that it was wrong'.

This, of course, was the classic test for insanity, which had been in use for many years, and in fact was the only test for insanity recognised by the law up until 1957. It was embodied in the McNaghten Rules. These said that, to be judged insane a defendant must not know the nature and quality of his act, or if he did know, did not know that it was wrong.

Both doctors commented on the fact that Revell's insanity was alcohol induced or alcohol aided. And this was reinforced by Revell's diary which was produced in court. The judge in his summing up drew the jury's attention to one passage in it where he wrote, 'DT's. Can see them coming through the wall at me'.

The jury were obviously influenced by the judge and the defence in their verdict. But the foreman made a mistake when he was asked for the verdict. He first of all said, 'Not guilty of murder' but then corrected it to 'Guilty of murder while insane'. Thus George Daniel Revell was sentenced to be detained during His Majesty's pleasure.

Bibliography

Books
David Boswell, *Sea Fishing Apprentices of Grimsby*, Grimsby Public Libraries and Museum, 1974
Robert Cecil, *Life in Edwardian England*, B.T. Batsford, 1969
B.J. Davey, *Rural Crime in the Eighteenth Century North Lincolnshire 1740-80*, The University of Hull Press, 1994
Alan Dowling, *Humberston Fitties*, Cleethorpes, 2001
Edward Drury, *The Great Grimsby Story*, Book 2 1870-1940, Edward Drury, 1985
Edward Drury, *The Greater Grimsby Story*, Book 3 1940-1990, Edward Drury, 1990
N.V. Gagen, *Hanged at Lincoln 1761-1961*, N.V. Gagen, 1998
Margaret Gerrish, *Before the Bulldozer*, NE Lincolnshire Council Library Services, 1998
Edward Gillett, *A History of* Grimsby, Oxford University Press, 1970
Adrian Gray, *Crime and Criminals in Victorian Lincolnshire*, Paul Watkins, 1993
David Kaye, *The Book of Grimsby*, Barracuda Books, 1981
Lincolnshire Federations of Women's Institutes, *Lincolnshire Villages*, Countryside Books, 2002
Geoffrey Moorhouse, *The Pilgrimage of Grace*, Weidenfeld & Nicholson, 2002
David N. Robinson, *The Book of the Lincolnshire Seaside*, Barron Books, 2000
Dave Wherry, *We Only Sing When We're Fishing*, Yore Publications, 2000

Directories
Great Grimsby and Cleethorpes Directory and Street Guide 1906-7, The Grimsby and Cleethorpes Directory Co.
Kelly's Directory of Lincolnshire 1909, Kelly's Directories Ltd

Maps and Newspapers
Grimsby (New Clee) 1906, Alan Godfrey Maps, 2000
Grimsby (North) 1906, Alan Godfrey Maps, 1999
Grimsby (South) 1906, Alan Godfrey Maps, 2000
Boston Gazette and Advertiser
Grimsby Evening Telegraph
Grimsby News
Lincolnshire Chronicle
Louth and North Lincolnshire Advertiser
Louth Standard
Stamford Mercury

If you are interested in purchasing other books published by The History Press, or in case you have difficulty finding any of our books in your local bookshop, you can also place orders directly through our website
www.thehistorypress.co.uk